The wellsprings of eternal joy

Translated from the French
Original title: «Aux sources inaltérables de la joie»

Original edition:
© 2005, Éditions Prosveta S.A., ISBN 2-85566-901-4

© Copyright Prosveta S.A. 2009. All rights reserved for all countries. No part of this publication may be reproduced, translated, adapted, stored in a retrieval system or transmitted, whether privately or otherwise, in any form or by any means, electronic, mechanical, photocopying, audio-visual or otherwise, without the prior permission of author and publishers (Law of March 1957 revised).

Prosveta S.A – B.P.12 – 83601 Fréjus CEDEX (France)

ISSN 0763-2738
ISBN 978-2-85566-976-2

Omraam Mikhaël Aïvanhov

The wellsprings of eternal joy

Izvor Collection – No. 242

PROSVETA

Readers are asked to note that Omraam Mikhaël Aïvanhov's teaching was exclusively oral. This volume includes passages from several different lectures all dealing with the same theme.

TABLE OF CONTENTS

Chapter One

GOD, THE BEGINNING AND END OF OUR JOURNEY

What do you suppose the inhabitants of other worlds know of the earth and its people? Not much. That is why, in certain regions of the universe, there are schools where teachers run courses for those who are curious about this motley crew known as human beings. First, they send deep-sea divers to plunge into our atmosphere, which is just as dark and opaque for them as the depths of the sea. Once there, they use fishing lines to capture a few specimens, which they take back to their laboratories. On class day, the teacher grabs some pincers and presents the 'catch' to his students. They are all delighted with the opportunity to make observations, followed by detailed reports and a commentary. And what comments they make!

Are some of you wondering whether I am serious? Of course not, don't worry! I know there is a lot written nowadays about extra-terrestrials coming in their flying saucers to abduct humans, whom they later do or don't return… Of course, creation being as rich and diverse as it is, many things are possible, but what I have read or heard up to now on this subject is certainly, in my opinion, the product of a great deal of imagination.

Entities in the invisible world that have been given the task of watching over the evolution of humanity have no need to come and collect a few specimens to take away and study goodness knows where. They know all about them, and yet they continue to find their mentality most peculiar. When European explorers discovered certain tribes in Africa or Oceania, they regarded them with such curiosity and amazement! Well, to these entities, humans appear even stranger, and what astonishes them the most is to see how they give their opinions and make judgments. They are ignorant, and yet they are ready to express an opinion on any subject whatsoever. So of course they make mistakes and suffer, but they carry on stubbornly, and the entities watching them are astounded and ask each other, 'How can we help them?'

The reason humans commit so many errors of judgment, behave so inappropriately and experience so much suffering is because they don't know what they have come to earth to do. They come and they go. In what cosmic plan is their destiny written? Where have they come from and what is their destination when they leave? They have no idea. There is only one answer to both questions: God. And in fact, that is our only certainty.

We have come from God, and we will one day return to God. What will happen to us between this point of departure and this return? Over the course of our numerous incarnations, what roads will we travel before we return to the source? That depends on us. God has prepared an exceptional destiny for us human beings. Every now and then we receive an intuition of it, a few fleeting visions, then the sky clouds over once more, and our uncertainties and tribulations begin all over again. But we must cling to these transient visions with all our might and never doubt their reality. All the things that can possibly happen to us on the way merely represent stages, and they must never efface or cause us to forget the vision of what we will be when we return to the bosom of the Eternal, enriched by our experiences and by the qualities and virtues we will have acquired and developed.

In all human beings, the true Self that aspires to the light is buried under the dust and debris of all that is not truly themselves. But one day, each of us will become as God wants us to be, as we already are in our higher self.[1] It is this certainty that gives meaning to everything we experience in life. Even if it is difficult, nothing must keep us from the path leading towards divine light, for the other paths will turn out to be even more difficult and painful.

The journey we undertook a long time ago will not end with our present life. This life is only one stage on the road all beings must travel once they have left the bosom of God. And how many different regions they will have to visit before returning to their place of origin! We are only travellers on earth, and we must never forget it. But even among people who are pursuing the spiritual life, very few are capable of holding onto the idea that they are travellers and must not stop anywhere and put down roots. The way is long, very long; we must constantly observe, study and draw conclusions so as to continue in the right direction, and in order not to lose heart we must keep our eyes fixed on our goal.

Watch the sun rise, allow yourself to be absorbed by this life, this brilliance, and your sensations will give you a foretaste of what you will experience when you return to God. In this great burst of light, in this radiance that is an expression of divine splendour, begin to seek your true self.[2] The day you discover this self and learn to identify with it, you will realize you have always lived in power, in love, in the light, and that through your life, through your activities, you are able to participate in the gigantic work that is taking place in the universe. And this is when the words of Jesus, *'My Father is still working, and I also am working'*, will become meaningful to you.[3]

How many people on earth do nothing, in fact, but destroy God's work! From the depths of the earth and the seas all the way to the stars, the creation is in constant motion, in perpetual transformation, and this is equally true of human souls. As often as you can, stop whatever you are doing for a few moments, and meditate on this divine activity that affects all regions of the universe simultaneously, that participates in the existence of all beings and satisfies all their needs. For God guarantees the present and future existence of all creatures, never forgetting a single one.

Whenever I travel and arrive in a new town, I see the crowds in the streets and remind myself that all of these men and women have their own lives, their history, their problems to resolve, their suffering, their loves, and that there is a Being who sustains them all because he lives in them. And you, too, try to hold this thought now and then, and you will enlarge your field of consciousness. You will discover new regions where you will enter into contact with higher entities.

Instead of troubling yourself with all sorts of useless or futile preoccupations that only weaken you, concentrate on the universal Spirit, the heavenly Father who created us, who keeps us, sustains us and lives within all his creatures. In doing so, you will escape the burden of everyday existence. You will sense that the link between your earthly being and your heavenly being is being restored, and one day, like Jesus, you will be able to say, *'My Father is still working, and I also am working'*.

At the moment, we know only the point of departure and the destination: God. Everything else is uncertain. But whatever happens to us along the path, we must continue to go forward, for only the divine life, the eternal life, is worthy of the name life.

You will say, 'But it is difficult, so difficult!' Yes, this is why you must never forget that you are inhabited by a spirit, by a spark that burst from the bosom of the Eternal, from the primordial Fire, and incarnated in matter. This spark carries all the divine blueprints within it, and all its peregrinations through matter have no other goal than to realize these plans. This spark needs food in order to stay alive, and one of the symbols of food, both physical and spiritual, is bread.

Jesus said, *'I am the living bread'*, *'I am the bread from heaven'*, and at the Last Supper he blessed the bread and gave it to his disciples, saying, *'Take, eat, this is my body'*.[4] Bread thus represents the elements of the divine life. When we come to earth we already possess certain of these elements. Those who have wasted them in their previous incarnations by living an unreasonable life must do their best to regain them; otherwise they will continue their journey amidst great difficulties.

In an initiatic school, all we are doing is filling our inner bags and granaries – that is to say our heart, mind, soul and spirit – with this living bread from heaven. I have often explained what this bread is, and also when to eat it and how to chew it.[5] It is available to us every day, enabling us to continue along the path that leads to our predestination as sons and daughters of God. The Lords of Destiny have provided everything we need to reach our goal. Perhaps they do not respond to the questions we ask, but this is only to keep us in suspense so that we never stop progressing.

Notes

1. See *Man's Psychic Life: Elements and Structures,* Izvor Coll. n° 222, chap. 13: 'The higher Self'.

2. See *Sunrise Meditations,* Brochure 323, and *'You are Gods',* part III, chap. 4: 'The sun, image of God and image of humankind'.
3. See *'Cherchez le Royaume de Dieu et sa Justice',* part VII: 'Mon Père travaille, et moi aussi je travaille avec Lui'.
4. See above, part VI, chap. 2-III: 'Celui qui mange ma chair et qui boit mon sang a la vie éternelle'.
5. See *'Know Thyself' – Jnana Yoga,* Part 1, Complete Works, vol. 17, chap. 2: 'The Synoptic Table' and chap. 6: 'Food for the soul and the spirit', and Part 2, Complete Works, vol. 18, chap. 4: 'Knowledge: heart and mind'; *Truth: Fruit of Wisdom and Love,* Izvor Coll. n° 234, chap. 3: 'Wisdom and love; light and warmth'.

Chapter Two

BEGINNING THE JOURNEY

Among all our possessions and all the beings we are attached to, nothing and no one truly and definitively belongs to us. Our money, our house, our job, health, friends and family – we could lose them at any time. When this happens, we have to call upon all our inner forces to help us bear the loss. And where can we find these forces? In light, disinterested love, humility and sacrifice. So why not consciously seek them right now? Why don't people choose to do this of their own free will instead of waiting until they are compelled by events?

People wait until they are destitute, ill or unhappy before they seek an inner direction, a spiritual orientation. When everything is going well, it is difficult to convince them they should concentrate on what is essential and prepare themselves for the ordeals to come. For they will come, that is certain. No one is spared, and if you are already well-armed, not only will you overcome them, you will emerge from them stronger than you were before.

Now, don't make the mistake of believing that a spiritual practice will deliver you from all evils.

It is preferable to be on the right path, but being on the right path doesn't mean you have reached your goal. On the one hand, it is true that certain types of suffering gradually disappear as you purify yourself and live in harmony with the world of light. But this doesn't mean that the consequences of the transgressions you have committed in this life or in previous lives will immediately be erased.

Don't be surprised if certain types of suffering refuse to leave you in spite of the new direction you have taken. Put simply, we can say that our good actions accumulate in one reservoir and our bad actions in another, and the good and bad inevitably catch up with us one day. So we pass through the events and the psychic and physical states that are the consequences of our behaviour in the distant and not so distant past.[1]

When you decide to embrace the spiritual life, the changes you provoke are inner ones. Externally, your existence will continue as before, with your particular family, social and professional environment, and with the same problems to be solved. And you will also have a physical body that is more or less healthy.

Let's take the example of health. There are physical weaknesses that a healthier lifestyle supported by a better philosophy quickly allows you to overcome. But there are also illnesses that are incurable, because their cause lies in the distant past and they are deeply engrained in your organism. The new life you have decided to lead can only give you methods that will enable you to deal more adequately with your deficient physical state and to plant seeds in yourself for future improvement; it cannot cure you from one day to the next.

It is important for the conduct of our daily life that we understand the significance of physical pain: it warns us that we have wandered from the right path. If we didn't suffer, we would run headlong into the grave. Nothing is more dangerous than an illness that takes hold in the organism without giving the slightest warning, for by the time the pain manifests and alerts us, the damage is often irreversible. So as soon as you feel a pain you must ask yourself what the cause is; try to discover what you may have done out of carelessness or negligence. If you pay no attention to these warnings, the illness you allow to take root in you will be increasingly difficult to fight.

If you are suffering from a serious illness, spiritual practices may not restore your health. Of course, faith and love are forces capable of overcoming illnesses considered incurable, but this happens only very rarely, since very few people have the faith in God and the love for him that are capable of working miracles.[2] Those content to lead a blameless life are able to prepare better conditions for their future, but that is all. In the present they reap the results of a defective past, but by living this present in the light they sow the seeds of a future incarnation. So the lives of disciples are a mixture of suffering and joy; they pay for their past transgressions but at the same time know they are creating their future.

Those who set out on the path of spirituality hoping to be spared life's ordeals must abandon their illusions. The spiritual life is not a bargain with the Lord. So they must not imagine that all of heaven will be so impressed to see them become members of a church or the Universal White Brotherhood or some other spiritual movement that it will come flying to their aid. They will still come up against all of life's difficulties, just as materialists do, but in spite of everything, they must continue to advance, knowing that these difficulties will purify and strengthen them, because they have learned to see them in a different light. By accepting a spiritual teaching, the poor do not become rich, the ignorant do not become erudite, the sick do not become fit and healthy, the weak do not become strong, and the despised and misunderstood do not receive honour and glory. So be warned! You may even feel poorer, weaker and more ignorant and lowly than before. Some of you who have experienced this tell me they don't understand what is happening to them. What can I say? Simply that the new life is beginning to circulate in them.

Yes, for this new, more intense life begins by refining your perception of your inner being, and it is normal not to feel very happy at first with what you discover. But at the same time your understanding expands, and this should make you happy. You say, 'But I'm not getting any freer, I'm not getting stronger!' How do you know? Since you were inactive before, you didn't have a clear idea of your abilities and could imagine you were powerful and free. But now you have decided to work, and the mediocre results of your first efforts force you to recognize your limitations. That is not a reason to become discouraged and stop working; little by little your strength will increase and your field of action will expand. But you must begin by seeing yourself as you are.

You have read Swift's Gulliver's Travels. After being shipwrecked at sea, Gulliver wakes up one morning on an unknown shore. And when he tries to get up, he realizes he is tied and bound: during his sleep, the country's tiny inhabitants, the Lilliputians, have lashed him to the ground with hundreds of little ropes.

Let's consider this adventure as an analogy of what happens in the spiritual life: if you haven't yet attempted to move, to get up, you don't know you are tied down. But as soon as you try to stand up and be on your way, you feel weak, paralyzed. A dog, horse or goat will be unaware of the rope tethering it to a stake until it tries to move about freely. And in the case of human beings, these ropes represent all the obscure tendencies that keep them fettered in lower states of consciousness.

Someone sitting comfortably in an armchair can imagine they are capable of all manner of exploits. It is only when they want to get up that they discover the true measure of their strength and are obliged to shed some illusions. Then, in their disillusionment, they believe themselves weaker than they actually are. No, on the contrary, this new awareness is the beginning of their strength. The difficulties they experience in distancing themselves from their past way of life are proof that they are trying to stir, to make some efforts. They suffer because they finally begin to sense the existence of a new world and to turn their life in that direction.

I want to make this very clear. Even though your decision to make efforts is commendable, you must also be aware of the upheavals this decision will produce in you. Otherwise you won't understand what is happening to you. You will return to your old life and will eventually have to begin all over again.

Take the example of people who for years have had a smoking habit. When they light up a cigarette they feel soothed, relaxed, as though smoking were good for their well-being, whereas in fact it is destroying their health. One day they finally understand it would be more intelligent to stop, but all the cells of their organism have become addicted to tobacco and rebel, clamour, sign petitions and nag until the person gives in.

Who hasn't heard of the endless struggles smokers or alcoholics have when they decide to get rid of their deadly habits? Why is it such a battle? Because our habits are ties we have created with living creatures – our cells – and to break these ties is very difficult, because our cells don't agree to it.[3] It is exactly like wanting to divorce a man or woman who refuses to separate. Deciding to change one's life is a heroic enterprise.

Tobacco, alcohol and drugs are examples everyone can easily understand. But it is the same for all bad habits and tendencies: faults, vices and even illnesses are entities living inside us endowed with their own will, which explains their resistance. This is also made clear in certain passages of the Gospels, which recount how Jesus drove out demons.[4]

Because he drove evil entities from their bodies, the demented regained their reason, the mute regained their speech and the paralyzed recovered the use of their limbs. But these entities don't accept defeat easily; they do everything they can to keep the upper hand. And Jesus explains, *'When the unclean spirit has gone out of a person, it wanders through waterless regions looking for a resting-place, but it finds none. Then it says, "I will return to my house from which I came." When it comes, it finds it empty, swept, and put in order. Then it goes and brings along seven other spirits more evil than itself, and they enter and live there; and the last state of that person is worse than the first.'*

Our weaknesses, like our virtues, are living entities that have chosen to make their home within us. As we make efforts to improve ourselves, these evil entities are forced to leave us, because our inner atmosphere becomes oppressive to them. They cannot bear the purity and light we are working to establish in ourselves, and they take flight. Once outside us, they look for new homes, entering other people, through whom they attempt to harm us. But this causes us less harm than when these entities occupied our dwelling.

And since we have defeated these enemies within, we are in a stronger position to conquer them outside ourselves. Will we ever succeed in getting rid of them once and for all? No, as long as we are on earth we will encounter difficulties and adversaries.

Why have so many remarkable people aroused such terrible hostility? Precisely because the dark forces they had driven from their inner world came back to attack them through other people, who were disturbed by their qualities, virtues and strength of character. People who live an ordinary life don't bother anyone; everyone is content with them. Once they decide to rid themselves of certain bad habits, however, the enemies they have driven out begin to attack them from without. But even if it is not easy to confront them, these external enemies are less dangerous than those within us.

So how should we act when faced with these external enemies? With love, gentleness and patience.[5] Yes, we should be firm, authoritative and severe with our inner enemies, but this is not a good method to use with our outer ones. Unfortunately, most of the time humans do just the opposite: they show patience and indulgence towards their inner enemies and extreme severity towards their external ones. Is it surprising, then, that they continue to struggle with inextricable difficulties?

Now I am going to tell you a Turkish story. Until the beginning of the twentieth century, Bulgaria was under Ottoman domination, so of course during that time there were many anecdotes in circulation, true or fictitious, in which the heroes were Turks.

Well, one day a wrestler of imposing size was strolling through a little street in Istanbul. His exploits had made him famous throughout the town, and he walked through the crowd with great pride… On his way he jostled a man walking in front of him, who cried out indignantly, 'Are you blind? Didn't you see someone walking in front of you? How dare you bump into a respectable man like me!' In response, the wrestler turned round, punched the man, knocking him to the ground and, unperturbed, continued on his way. A few moments later he overtook another man and jostled him in the same way. But this one looked at him without anger and said, 'I am very happy to meet you. It is a great honour to be knocked about by a champion like you.' The wrestler drew a purse full of silver coins from his pocket and said to him, 'Here, this is for you! I reward the wise. The others I throw to the ground.'

Is this story true or not? It doesn't matter. It is very interesting from a symbolic point of view. On the road of life, we are often knocked about by difficult events and situations, but it is useless to protest and sound off indignantly, saying, 'What! How dare you do that to me!' because this is the best way to ensure you will continue to receive blows and be thrown to the ground. On the other hand, those who think it is a blessing to be knocked about will always gain something: they will acquire experience and become stronger and richer.

In a certain sense, we can consider the reactions of these two passers-by as manifestations of our two natures: our lower nature, thin-skinned and vindictive, and our higher nature, which sees in every difficulty an opportunity to perfect itself.[6] Whenever you find yourself in a difficult or humiliating situation, remember these two Turks, jostled by a wrestler in the streets of Istanbul. The first suffered two defeats: he didn't know how to resist the injunctions of his lower nature that drove him to retaliate, and on top of that he was thrown to the ground. As for the second, he won two victories: he listened to the advice of his higher nature and received a purse full of silver coins.

Notes

1. See *Man, Master of his Destiny,* Izvor Coll. n° 202, chap. 8: 'Reincarnation'.
2. See *Love Greater than Faith,* Izvor Coll. n° 239, chap. 4: 'Your faith has made you well'.
3. See *'You are Gods'*, part IX, chap. 4: 'The body of glory', pp. 534-540.
4. See *Life Force,* Complete Works, vol. 5, chap. 7: 'Unwanted guests'.
5. See *'Cherchez le Royaume de Dieu et sa Justice',* part V, chap. 2: 'Aimez vos ennemis'.
6. See *Man's Two Natures, Human and Divine,* Izvor Coll. n° 213.

Chapter Three

SUFFERING IS A STIMULUS

What do most religions have to say about suffering? That it comes from God: that God sends trials and tribulations to the just because he loves them, and he notes down everything the wicked do so that he can punish them for their faults and force them back onto the right path. But is it really God who sends suffering to people, good or bad?

A child calls out to his mother in tears. She rushes to him, and the child says, ‘It’s Toto’s fault.’

‘Ah’, she replies. ‘What happened?’

‘I wanted to ride his bike, and he wouldn’t lend it to me. So I tried to take it from him, but I slipped and banged my head against the wall. Toto is so mean.’ The child hurt himself trying to take his friend’s bicycle, but this is his friend’s fault, not his.

A woman falls in love with her friend’s husband and cannot accept that this man, who in her opinion should belong to her, is tied to another. So of course she suffers. But instead of recognizing she has put herself in an impossible situation, she allows herself to be devoured by jealousy. She ponders her revenge and turns her life into a living hell.

So much of the suffering people complain about is no different from these examples! People want to take what belongs to others: objects, property, husbands, wives, jobs and so on, and of course it is the others who are at fault, because they are blocking the satisfaction of their desires and ambitions. So how can they free themselves from this suffering if they never understand it is they themselves who have caused it? God has nothing to do with it.

All human beings will experience this kind of suffering until they also understand that nothing they possess or hope to possess can ever give them security. People suffer because they are penniless, weak, ill, ignorant, ugly or alone; but having wealth, power, health, knowledge, beauty and the company of lots of people has never prevented anyone from suffering. In fact, we are often astonished to discover the inner torments and struggles of men and women who seem to have everything they need to be happy.

As I have told you, those who decide to give priority to acquiring spiritual riches cannot avoid certain suffering, but they become free. On the other hand, those who think only of increasing their bank balance, their social influence, their power over others in fact only limit themselves inwardly. And even if at first they draw great satisfaction from these things, sooner or later they will be forced by circumstances to accept external limitations as well. So they will suffer, and this suffering brings nothing good with it, neither for themselves nor for others; it only makes them bitter and mean. Who willingly gives up what they have spent so much time and energy acquiring?

Occasionally, the soul of someone who has sought only material satisfactions is softened in the long run by great suffering, but this is rare. On the other hand, the suffering experienced by those who walk the path of spiritual growth increases their love and light. This suffering is comparable to that of a woman giving birth to a baby. Her child is the fruit of a long gestation, and it often comes into the world amidst great pain, but what joy there is when it finally arrives! Christianity takes inspiration from this experience when it teaches that the goal of the spiritual life is to give birth to the Christ Child within every human being.[1]

You must avoid exposing yourself to the sort of suffering that limits you; the law of evolution makes no provision for this suffering. It isn't God who sends this to people; it is they themselves, in their ignorance, who create it and who multiply it by repeating their mistakes. They complain, they wail, but if someone delivers them from this suffering they always manage to attract more. You could say they cannot do without it. Of course they won't admit this, but it is true nevertheless. Peace and serenity are foreign to them; they are bored and don't know how to fill their time, and they rush back to activities that will make them suffer once again.

Yes, just think about it: first one war, then another, and still another break out in various parts of the world. Everyone deplores the fact and wonders why there are so many of them… But it is simply because humans don't know how to take advantage of the good conditions that peace provides.[2] It takes great science to determine how people should occupy themselves in peacetime. Besides, even during times of peace, people continue to be at war. We see nothing but rivalry in every sphere of life: politics, business, finance, religion and even the family are fields of conflict, absolute battlegrounds. How can we be surprised when armed conflict breaks out everywhere, bringing so much unhappiness in its wake? And then everyone begs the Lord to put an end to these wars and restore peace. But I ask you, what does all this have to do with the Lord? What a strange notion people have of him!

You must learn to distinguish between two kinds of suffering, so that you are able to avoid the kind that indicates you have taken the wrong path and, on the other hand, to accept the kind you necessarily encounter as you advance on the path of good. Of course, at the time you are suffering it isn't always easy to discern the nature of this suffering, nor whether it is constructive or destructive. But you know the criteria, and if you have learnt to analyse yourself you will quickly realize which is which.

Now, just because I tell you that suffering is an inevitable part of our evolution, it doesn't mean you should create opportunities for yourself to suffer and become unhappy. Suffering accompanies all evolution and we cannot avoid it, but it is useless and even dangerous to try to add to it. Many monks and ascetics have seriously misunderstood this question of suffering and have voluntarily inflicted all sorts of torments on themselves 'to please God', so they thought! As if God took pleasure in seeing the human creature wounded and bleeding! But there are very few religions that have not recommended this type of practice in the past, and some still do today.

It is time we understood that the Lord has no need for people to suffer. The era of flagellation, self-torture and martyrdom has passed. Mistreating and mutilating the body, risking or destroying one's life: this way of offering oneself in sacrifice to the Lord is totally useless. True sacrifice lies in disinterested, brotherly love for all human beings. Those who have understood the meaning and power of love have no need to inflict suffering on themselves: they will get plenty of it from sharing in other people's misery! And the obstacles they encounter in their efforts to help others will give them even more opportunity to suffer! But they must not shrink from this kind of suffering, for it will make them grow and become nobler.

Those who love others and sincerely want to help them are obligated every day to shed a little more of their egoism and self-interest. Good intentions and feelings are not enough; there is a whole work of adjustment to be done, and this work is difficult. Why do so many people become discouraged by the difficulties they encounter in their efforts to help others? Because they have not understood that helping others demands the greatest abnegation.

No human being on earth is exempt from suffering. But we must know that some suffering is useful, beneficial, and others are unnecessary, useless and even dangerous. Unnecessary suffering is what we ourselves create by transgressing the laws of honesty, justice, goodness, wisdom and love. It doesn't deserve much compassion, for it resembles the suffering of the wolf, when it cannot pounce on the sheep which are protected by the shepherd, or that of the fox eyeing the chickens safe in their henhouse. All the same, this type of suffering is useful for those who know how to draw lessons from it: they understand they must orient their thoughts, feelings and desires more positively if they are to avoid destroying themselves.

Everyone will experience suffering; this is inevitable. But the malicious, who suffer because they stubbornly persist in their malice, lose something, whereas the benevolent, who suffer as they persevere along the path of goodness, are enriched by their suffering. Look at the faces of those who are jealous and envious: their frustrations are etched in their sombre, tense, troubled features. And then look at those who have suffered and sacrificed for great causes: even if they haven't been understood, their ordeals have ennobled them and made them more beautiful. They have discovered whole new worlds within themselves and have acquired true strength.

Unalterable laws govern the universe created by God, including the way it functions and its evolution. Human beings are part of this universe, and if they transgress the laws, they collide with cosmic forces and receive blows.[3] So in a certain sense it is true: we can say that God is punishing them. And if they continually make the effort to improve their understanding and respect for these laws, the difficulties they encounter will also cause them to suffer. But the kind of suffering they inevitably encounter on the path of evolution contributes to their development. This is why we can equally say that God makes the just suffer because he loves them. It is his love that desires their growth and blossoming, and this love is part of cosmic law.

It is up to human beings to choose the form of suffering they consider most beneficial to them. To avoid it should never be a goal, for suffering forces us to progress, and there is always progress to be made. It is true that suffering can make people malicious, but not suffering can do the same. It is difficult for those who have never suffered to understand the suffering of others, and they can be impatient and cruel towards them. Feelings open the door to reflection, and certain painful feelings compel us to draw closer and closer to what is essential. In reality, suffering is a goad, a stimulus: it not only puts us back on the right path when we have gone astray, it forces us to go ever further and higher.

Master Peter Deunov said, ‘Must you cry when it’s time to wash your shirt? Must you cry when it’s time to plant seeds in the ground? Must you cry when it's time to grind the wheat?' Washing your shirt, planting seeds and grinding wheat correspond to activities of the spiritual life. Which ones? To wash your shirt is to purify yourself. To plant seeds in the soil is to introduce good thoughts and feelings into your mind and heart, and also into the minds and hearts of others. And to grind wheat is to prepare the bread of life. These three activities are accompanied by certain suffering, but such salutary suffering! It is this divine suffering, consciously accepted, that imbues all our experiences thereafter with beauty, fragrance and flavour.

Notes

1. See *Noël et le mystère de la naissance du Christ,* Brochure 321.
2. See *The Egregor of the Dove or the Reign of Peace,* Izvor Coll. n° 208, chap. 1: 'Towards a better understanding of peace'.
3. See *Cosmic Moral Law,* Complete Works, vol. 12, chap. 7: 'The laws of nature and moral law'.

Chapter Four

SEEKING GOD'S ANSWERS WITHIN

Why is it that so many believers lose their faith? Because in most cases it doesn't help them through their difficulties. The religious doctrines they are asked to accept blindly are of no help to them, so little by little their faith becomes like a fraying garment. There is no point telling them they will find the answer in religion: they feel lost and empty.[1] And it is useless to try and convince them of the opposite of what they feel, since no argument is effective when it goes against people's feelings.

Several times during their life, people experience great difficulties that force them to ask themselves the only truly important questions about the meaning of life. And even if they sincerely turn towards religion at such times, they often find the answers it offers inadequate, ridiculous or even monstrous. A mother and father, for instance, watch their child die, and they ask themselves, 'But why? Why?' What comfort can they find in the words of someone who replies, 'It's the will of God'? Was it God's will for their child to fall ill and die? Was it God's wish for him to be killed one evening in a road accident after drinking too much with his friends? Did God want him to take drugs or commit suicide?

People must now be given true knowledge, initiatic knowledge; otherwise, whatever is done, the word 'religion' will lose all meaning for them. And besides, more and more we are seeing that it is doctors, nurses, psychologists and psychiatrists, not priests or pastors, who are helping people through the ordeals in their lives.

It can also happen that, when they are overwhelmed by suffering, some people delve so deeply within themselves that they find the answers there. It is neither religion nor belief that helps them; they find faith within themselves, thanks to the experience they are going through. For the truth is, God has placed within human beings all the answers to the questions they ask themselves, as well as all the resources they need to confront life's difficulties. They can eventually find these through trial and error, and they are even more likely to find them this way than through the ready-made words of the religious.

Of course, it is when people are suffering that they pose most questions about the existence and will of God. And above all, they ask, 'Will he come to my aid?' But they receive no response. Why? Because they ask this question as though God were a being completely outside themselves. Once they understand that God lives within them, and if through all their ordeals they continue to link themselves to this God within, then yes, they will sense that he guides them, enlightens them and sustains them.

When people suffer they often feel very alone, abandoned by everyone. Why then, through ignorance and neglect, must they also lose the only real support, the only real comfort available to them? This support and comfort are found in the presence of God within them. And when they pray, they not only address the Creator of heaven and earth, a Being so remote they cannot even imagine him, but also a power that dwells within them, with which they will never again lose contact.[2]

It is understandable that in their distress men and women consult the clergy, doctors and psychologists and even feel the need to turn to radio and television. The responses they receive will depend on the quality of those they consult. But they must know that the real answers to their questions lie within them, waiting to be discovered. So while continuing to question others, if that makes them feel better, they should make the effort to search within themselves, in their soul and spirit, for they will only obtain true answers when they learn to consult their inner God.

In reality, you receive answers to all your questions, to all your prayers. If you don't hear them it is because you have surrounded yourself with impenetrable walls by entertaining thoughts, feelings, desires and actions that were not inspired by love, wisdom and truth. But once you begin to bring these walls down you will receive replies, sometimes even before you have formulated the question.[3]

Here is how you can verify what I am telling you. Address your question to this being within you that knows everything: to your higher self, which is a representative of God himself. Ask your question with complete sincerity and trust, and then forget about it. Sooner or later the response will come. It will be brought to you in a dream or in an encounter with someone who most likely knows nothing of what worries or torments you. Or it will come through something you read, a work of art you go to hear or see, or a natural phenomenon. But you must have eyes that observe and ears that listen. If you are conscious and vigilant, you will be astonished by the answers the invisible world is capable of giving you through other people, animals or even plants, as well as through objects you once considered foreign, indifferent, mute, lifeless.

But you must also know that the response you receive will not necessarily be easy to accept. When you are struggling in an impossible situation and wonder how you will ever get out of it, you tend to think the solution will appear and free you, as if someone had waved a magic wand. No, the solution may demand great efforts of you. But don't turn back, for if this really is the solution, painful though it may be, it is worth more than all the hesitation, uncertainty and anguish you have been suffering until now.

Notes

1. See *The Faith that Moves Mountains,* Izvor Coll. n° 238, chap. 3: 'Faith and belief' and chap. 7: 'A religion is only one form of faith'.
2. See above, chap. 9: 'Proof of God's existence lies within us' and chap. 10: 'Identifying with God'.
3. See *Looking Into the Invisible,* Izvor Coll. n° 228, chap. 7: 'Messages from heaven'.

Chapter Five

IN THE SCHOOL OF LIFE: THE LESSONS OF COSMIC INTELLIGENCE

What we call ordeals are nothing but a series of problems we have to resolve throughout the course of our lives, just as school children and university students have problems to solve. As they gradually progress, they are given increasingly difficult exercises and are asked to study their subjects in greater depth. Of course they will leave school or university one day, but no one ever leaves the school of life.

The exercises and efforts required of human beings over the course of their lives will therefore be endless. So instead of complaining and protesting about having yet another burden to carry or another obstacle to overcome, they must first understand why they have these tests and what they mean, and then rejoice at having new experiences to live and new truths to discover, for these experiences and these truths are the only true riches. If, after an ordeal, their strength, faith and love have grown, it means they have passed their exam well, and this greater strength, faith and love are like their diplomas.

Judging by the usual reactions and behaviour of some people, you would think they experienced life as the work of a hostile divinity seeking to destroy them. Life is the most powerful force there is, but it has no wish to annihilate humans. The difficulties and obstacles we find on our path are there to make us stronger, not to destroy us, and it is up to us to appease this force we call life by learning to work with it.[1]

How do we explain that what is difficult and painful for some is neither difficult nor painful for others? It is just like at school, where certain pupils finish an exercise in a few minutes and receive an excellent mark, while others struggle, fail to finish the task and get a miserable mark. And if, instead of facing up to their problems by seeking the solutions within themselves, people are content simply to ignore them, to run away from them or hold others responsible, life will catch up with them later on, and they will have more and more trouble resolving them. Again, just like at school! This explains why, when they are in difficulty, those who are weak or lazy and already impoverished lose something, whereas those who work and are already rich gain even more.

I have sometimes pointed out to you the analogy between our inner difficulties and a swamp. As long as the swamp hasn't been drained, we live in a fog and are attacked by mosquitoes, because the swamp provides the best conditions for their proliferation. And our life is nothing but an endless struggle against fog and mosquitoes.

When you see certain people wrestling for years with the same unsolvable problems, day after day exhibiting the same anxieties and repeating the same complaints, you would like to help them to free themselves of all this, but how? You talk to them, you explain to them that their external conditions won't change, that it is up to them to change, but to no avail; they remain in their swamp with their mosquitoes.[2]

As I speak, I'm sure each of you is thinking of at least one person you know, since it is easier to recognize what goes on in others than in oneself. And yet everyone is living through this kind of situation – to a greater or lesser extent, to be sure, but each of us has swamps that need to be drained and filled so that mosquitoes, in other words our worries and suffering, no longer have a home in us.

Too often we seek external solutions to our problems instead of trying to confront them within ourselves and bring them fully into the light. We can compare this attitude to that of a mother who has to discipline a disobedient child. Instead of trying to understand the reasons for his behaviour (for there is certainly something to understand), she gives him a few smacks to keep him quiet. In doing so, she uses the easiest method, and the child will continue to disobey her. Well, we must understand that from a certain point of view our problems are also our children, and according to how we deal with them, either we will solve them or we won't!

From the moment we arrive on earth, life undertakes to instruct us, to force us to find the best ways to manifest ourselves. No one can escape earth's laws.

You will say, 'And what about very evolved beings, initiates and masters?' They cannot escape these laws either. They arrive imbued with the emanations of heaven, but earth is a completely different world. Matter is so opaque, so difficult to work with, that for them as well as for others it represents an obstacle. On the subtle planes on high, matter is obedient, malleable, and it submits to the slightest thought, the slightest desire. But the matter we live in offers the greatest resistance.[3]

In sending us to earth, where we will always have obstacles to surmount and ordeals to overcome, Cosmic Intelligence gives us the opportunity to unfold and blossom here in matter. For obstacles and ordeals are also matter, a type of matter. And if, when faced with difficulties, you are able to think, 'There is no point moaning and groaning. I'm going to study how this Intelligence works', you will be filled with such wonder that you will endure your difficulties much more easily. This is a new way of seeing things, as the most common attitudes in the face of ordeals are obviously rebellion, anger or despair.

All children cry at birth, but they don't all cry in the same way. Some make a touching, plaintive sound, expressing nostalgia for the region of light, joy and peace they have left behind. But at the same time they are saying, 'May God's will be done!' and they accept in advance the ordeals that await them. Whereas, many others wail in a desperate, tragic way, crying out in rebellion, because they feel like animals caught in a trap and already know their lives will be like prisons.

On earth no one is spared, precisely because it is earth, and very specific conditions apply here. So we must learn how best to avoid being crushed by events and instead master them and draw from them what is best for our evolution.

There are more difficulties to be dealt with on the mental plane than on the astral plane, and more on the astral plane than on the physical plane. The difference is that obstacles on the physical plane are visible, tangible, palpable and obvious. But in fact everything begins on the plane of thought, so this is where we must begin to try to resolve problems, not on the physical plane, where they have already materialized.

Of course, you will not succeed immediately in changing your reactions to what happens to you. You will always begin by feeling shaken, upset, shocked. Yes, but once you have understood that these difficulties are necessary to your apprenticeship, you will regain your strength and confidence much more quickly and effectively.

So begin by deciding never to complain, never to believe that destiny is bent on your destruction. And don't imagine that you would be happier if your life were easy and smooth. No, with an easy, problem-free life you would simply stagnate. If you want to advance and make yourself useful, you must come to understand the wisdom with which Cosmic Intelligence has created nature and human beings, and you will see what responses it gives you.

Suppose you want to climb a mountain. Could you reach the summit if the slopes of this mountain were smooth? No, it would be impossible to get a foothold anywhere, and you would slip. It is thanks to the rough places that you manage to hoist yourself to the top. How many times have I told you this! Cosmic Intelligence has left indicators everywhere in the universe, signs to help us find our way, showing us how to progress, how to work. But those who never learn to decipher them discover nothing; they simply suffer.

And why don't they learn to decipher these messages? Because they are obsessed with their desire to obtain what suits and pleases them. They don't know that, in order to have a better understanding of things, they mustn't harbour such desires and lusts in their heart and mind, for these desires and lusts tie them down and limit them. Once they possess true light they will understand how their difficulties and obstacles, which they can't escape in any case, help them to advance and grow.

Would you like more examples? Well, consider this: why is it that human beings have no difficulty moving over the ground? Because the ground is hard, it offers resistance. If you try to move on quicksand, you become bogged down and are eventually engulfed. And how is it that boats can move over the water? Because water is also resistant. It isn't as resistant as earth, of course, but all the same, it is thanks to this liquid medium that boats can advance. And it is also thanks to the resistance of air that aeroplanes can take off and fly in the sky.

You see, whether on earth, on water or in the air, it is only because of resistance that we can move, that we can advance. And it is the same in the psychic domain. Once you have understood the usefulness of difficulties and obstacles, not only will you no longer complain, you will thank heaven, saying, ‘Here is a magnificent opportunity to progress’, and you will feel lighter, you will smile, and you will even feel proud of yourself. There are laws you have to know if you are to progress. You will say you can also choose not to progress. Yes, of course, but then you will be crushed, trampled, because to progress, to move forward, is the law of life.

Continue to question Cosmic Intelligence and it will also give you the example of powder. Where does gunpowder’s force come from? From the fact that it is compressed. Well, in the same way, when life imposes limitations on us and confines us by means of our difficulties, we concentrate extraordinary forces within ourselves so that we can surmount our obstacles. Without these difficulties we would do nothing; people who are satisfied fall asleep.

Sometimes you feel the need to melt into the universal soul, to contemplate the immensity of the sea or a starry sky and immerse yourself in them. But if you remain in this state of expansion and dispersion you will achieve nothing on earth. In order to act, you must use the law of condensation, of concentration.

We need great expanses of sky and sea in order to expand, and then a tiny space in order to concentrate, to gather our forces and act. It is in our ordeals that we find this tiny space.

An ordeal constrains us, and we must not complain about it but instead try to understand its meaning. Conflicts, obstacles and restrictions force us to fall back on our resources, to concentrate our energies and forces. Concentration and dispersion correspond to the two astrological signs, Capricorn and Leo. Leo is an externalizing sign: it projects, dispenses. Capricorn, on the other hand, is an internalizing sign: it accumulates and condenses. Under its influence in December and January, the earth concentrates energies in the roots of the trees in preparation for the explosion of life in July and August, for the abundance of fruit under the influence of Leo.

Life subjects us to great pressures so that we amass and condense our strength and our energy. What would we be capable of doing if we remained dispersed? In the same way, when we are faced with an obstacle, we concentrate, we pull ourselves together, step back a little… and then leap! Obstacles only appear to oppose us. They are there to force us to surmount them and grow stronger.

You will say, 'But I want space, I want freedom!' Well yes, so do I, but true space and freedom are only given to us after a great many compressions and constraints. When we are compressed on the physical and psychic planes, our spirit rejoices; it is jubilant because it can finally exercise its power over matter.

We are on earth, and earth is not this garden of delights we call paradise. We are treated harshly here. We must begin to work, otherwise we will continue to ask questions and never have answers. In humanity's present state, no one can avoid ordeals; they are part of our evolution. They vary from person to person, depending on one's age, life conditions and degree of evolution, but no one can escape them.

Children and adults, students and teachers, rich and poor, citizens and leaders all have ordeals to endure, for everyone has something that needs to be understood. Those who learn how to pass through these difficult periods when absolutely nothing is working, when they are harassed and overburdened, gain infinitely more than if they had gone from triumph to triumph. But for this to happen, you must not see only the negative side of the situation, or you poison yourself, you gnaw away at yourself and become bitter, you no longer believe in anything and even become spiteful and cruel.

The moment a trial presents itself, concentrate, reflect and pray in order to find the methods, the energy and, above all, the light you need. Instead of complaining and drowning in your sorrows, say to yourself, 'This is a good time to start building something solid and unshakeable in myself.'

And don't wait until you find yourself in great difficulty before making this kind of resolution.

You must be vigilant each day, with every little disappointment, every little disillusionment, every little blow to your pride. Instead of saying to yourself, 'Why has something like this happened to me? I don't deserve to be treated this way,' seize this opportunity to do some work on yourself. Don't let the chance slip by, and remember these lessons from Cosmic Intelligence.

The Master Peter Deunov said, 'Suffering is for human beings what the natural conditions of growth and development are for plants. The soul that suffers gives forth flowers that will one day become fruits. A soul that does not suffer remains a closed bud. So nourish your soul with the ripe fruits of your life and you will gain your freedom.' What does this mean?

In life we have a choice between two attitudes: the lazy attitude of those who are content to remain within their comfort zone, where they doze and stagnate, and that of the awakened and courageous beings who have resolved to grow in the light, whatever their difficulties. They are like plants: fixed in the soil, they are forced to endure heat and cold, wind and storms. These are certainly painful conditions, but in spite of them they grow and blossom. And how beautiful their colours are, and how lovely their fragrances!

Symbolically, people on the spiritual path are exposed to the same difficult conditions as plants. And yet these conditions are far preferable to those experienced by lazy people, who choose to remain sheltered in their 'granary'. In the granary, of course, seeds are not exposed to bad weather, but they risk other dangers that are far more serious: they may go mouldy, be devoured by mice or grubs and, above all, serve no useful purpose. The worst of all destinies is to be useless! When planted in the soil of the spiritual life, human beings come up against obstacles, but at least they are on the right path: they grow, they defend themselves, they create.

For you as a disciple, as for the seed, it is better to suffer exposure to all kinds of weather than to stagnate in a granary where, little by little, life will eventually leave you. You must not imagine that by seeking to preserve your life you will protect it.[4] On the contrary, life in the indolent dwindles on its own. Try an experiment: sow some seeds you have kept for a long time. They will fail to germinate, because their life has slipped away.

We must take the seeds already accumulated within us and sow them without delay, or they will lose all their qualities. So many people stuff their granary – their head – with all sorts of knowledge, which they allow to grow mouldy or to dry out with inertia, inactivity and uselessness! It is all very well to accumulate knowledge, but only on condition that you sow it, in other words put it into practice so it will grow and bear fruit. And we can only make it grow and bear fruit by putting it to the test of life.

In order to progress, to grow and become stronger, we must know how to confront our difficulties. Those who seek a life of ease out of a fear of suffering will encounter other, greater difficulties, and in any case they won't avoid suffering, as it is their life itself they are in the process of wasting.

Meditate on the long adventure of a grain of wheat before it becomes the bread that nourishes human beings. It is planted in the dark, cold earth, where it dies giving birth to a new sprout. When the sprout emerges from the earth, it discovers air and light and becomes a fine ear of wheat. But then comes harvest time: the ears are reaped and then threshed, for the grain must be separated from the chaff. And its suffering doesn't end here, for the grain is now taken to the mill to be ground and transformed into flour. One day the baker adds water to the flour, kneads it until it becomes a smooth dough and moulds it into the shape of a loaf. It is then time for the trial by fire: the bread is put in the oven. When baked to a golden brown, it is brought to the table and delivered up to the teeth of human beings. Still more suffering! And yet the grain is happy. Why? Because it is serving as nourishment.

So now let's interpret the grain of wheat's adventure. What does it have to do with us? Each stage of its transformation has its equivalent in our inner life. All these ordeals serve to make us grow, ripen and 'cook' until we are ready to be taken to the Lord's table to be 'eaten' by him and 'inhaled' by him.[5] For scents are also a form of food. Before eating a piece of fruit, begin by inhaling its fragrance. At least for a few moments, this will be enough; you won't feel the need to eat the fruit right away.

Sometimes, in the grip of unbearable suffering, people are wrenched from themselves and experience a sort of ecstasy, for suffering at its most intense can give birth to the purest joy. Extreme suffering verges on ecstasy, and the more acute the suffering, the more intense the ecstasy. Martyrs have experienced such ecstasy, born of their suffering. But people capable of attaining this state of separation from themselves are rare.

Knowing how to suffer is to possess some of the greatest knowledge there is. It is one of the highest manifestations of love. Through this suffering the soul prepares a fragrance so delectable that the Lord and his angels come to delight in it. From the suffering of the saints and martyrs, condemned and persecuted for the glory of God, an actual fragrance emanates. And the suffering, accepted with love by those who dedicate themselves to others, who sacrifice themselves in order to illuminate others and protect them from evil, as Jesus did, exudes the subtlest fragrance.

Accept this truth, put it into practice, and you will possess unparalleled strength. First of all, stop crying out at the slightest disappointment, the slightest ordeal. Accept it consciously in silence, and out of this suffering you will bring joy.

If the Lord is our nourishment, we are also his. And we are also nourishment for all those around us. Their intellect, their heart, their soul and their spirit are nourished by our qualities and virtues.

Notes

1. See *The Faith that Moves Mountains,* Izvor Coll. n° 238, chap. 11: 'God is life'.
2. See *The Living Book of Nature,* Izvor Coll. n° 216, chap. 3: 'Spring water or stagnant water'.
3. See *'Cherchez le Royaume de Dieu et sa Justice',* part II, chap. 4: 'Du soleil à la terre: comment la pensée se réalise dans la matière'.
4. See *Sons and Daughters of God,* Izvor Coll. n° 240, chap. 3: 'Whoever would save his life will lose it'.
5. See *The Philosopher's Stone – in the Gospels and in Alchemy,* Izvor Coll. n° 241, chap. 4: 'But if the salt loses its flavour...'

Chapter Six

'LIKE A FISH IN WATER'

‘Like a fish in water’… You have heard this expression, which means one has found one’s element. Out of water a fish suffers; it struggles and suffocates, because its respiratory system only functions in water, not in air.

So many human beings are like fish out of water! They feel ill at ease, strangers in their environment, so as soon as they can they leave their family, go off to another country or live completely on the margins of society. But it isn’t always possible to leave your family, your country or society, and most people continue to suffer in conditions they find suffocating.

Take the professional life, for example: someone who would like to have pursued studies in philosophy ends up working in a factory; someone with artistic leanings ends up becoming an accountant or a lawyer; and someone who needs to live in the open air is shut inside all week in a shop or office… In fact, you know more about this subject than I do. But I also know something about it, because there are people who don’t feel comfortable where they are and also don't know what they are suited for, and they come and ask me for advice.

In reality, the question confronting human beings doesn't only concern their physical or social position; not only their heart and intellect but also their soul and spirit must find the right conditions for their full development. The situation of a king in his palace seems so enviable! But if he has no interest in hearing his ministers report on the state of the kingdom, if receiving ambassadors from foreign countries bores him, and if he only enjoys the hunt or the flowers and trees in his magnificent gardens, he is unhappy. As you know, making locks was said to be the favourite pastime of King Louis XVI.

This reminds me of a Bulgarian tale. One day a prince was walking through his kingdom when he met a gypsy begging at the roadside. She was dressed in rags, and over her shoulder she held a long stick from which hung an even longer bag. In spite of her rags, the prince saw that she was very beautiful, and he fell in love with her and married her. Of course, the silks and velvets, the pearls and precious stones she was adorned with from that time on made her beauty all the more dazzling. But soon the prince noticed something strange: the princess tended to disappear from time to time. 'But where does she go? What does she do?' he wondered.

One day, he decided to solve this mystery and secretly arranged to follow her. He saw her go through a hidden door into a room in her apartment, where she locked herself in. He waited a moment and then, consumed with curiosity, peeked through the keyhole. And what did he see? The princess had smeared her face with soot and had exchanged her magnificent garments for her old rags. She was carrying her bag over her shoulder and walking with huge steps, brandishing her stick to chase away a band of imaginary dogs. She needed to take on her bohemian appearance again from time to time in order to endure her existence as a woman who had everything.

And here is a story that is completely true. During my youth in Bulgaria, I lived in the town of Varna. An old beggar used to stand by the entrance of a church, and I used to go and talk to him from time to time with one of my friends. He described so many beautiful things to us, which is why we enjoyed listening to him, in spite of his dirtiness and his unkempt hair, beard and moustache. One day we told ourselves we couldn't leave such a nice man in such a terrible situation: we had to do something for him.

I knew a woman in a position to intervene for him with the government. Among other things, she had translated books by the French astronomer Camille Flammarion into Bulgarian. So my friend and I went to tell her about this case. She promised to do something, and that was how, soon afterwards, the beggar found himself clean and properly dressed, living in one of the town's homes for the aged where he lacked for nothing. We were very pleased, so you can imagine how surprised we were one day to find he had escaped from the home and returned to begging at the church entrance! What a lesson for us! Yes, one's place… in what situation do people feel they are truly in the right place?

But just because someone is suffering in a particular situation, it doesn't always mean he or she has the opportunity or the right to change it. It is the laws of karma, the laws of destiny, that determine people's place, in accordance with what they deserve or what is best for their evolution. If they escape to a place they find more desirable, more comfortable, they will only make matters worse for themselves. Someone who manages by devious means to take the place reserved for someone more deserving will have to leave it one way or another, and someone who remains modestly in the shadows may be called to fill the highest of positions.

At the theatre, sometimes ill-mannered members of the audience will seat themselves in the first row, hoping no one will come and make them move. But the usher arrives, asks to see their tickets and sends them to the gallery, and those who have reserved the seats come to take their rightful places. Well, the same thing happens in life. So if someone has momentarily taken the place that is rightfully yours, don't worry, the 'usher' will come and chase the usurper away. Yes, in the great theatre of life, each of us receives a number corresponding to our allotted place, and it is up to us to discover and interpret this number.

Like the fish in water, the mole under ground, the bird in the air and the salamander (so they say) in the fire, every creature must find its right place. And what is that place for human beings? Their place is the entire universe, and the different bodies which go to make them up are linked with the four elements: the physical body with earth, the heart with water, the intellect with air and the soul and spirit with fire.[1]

It isn't enough to find one's place in a family, a country or a profession. If the heart, intellect, soul and spirit haven't also found the place where they receive the nourishment they need, a person will always feel dissatisfied. The heart needs warmth and love, the intellect needs light and wisdom, the soul needs immensity and the spirit eternity. But under the pressure of certain circumstances, your heart may lose its warmth, your intellect may become clouded, your soul constricted and your spirit paralysed. When that happens, the only solution is to make a move so as to give each of your faculties the conditions needed for its unfolding, and this change in location is called reflection, meditation, prayer, contemplation or identification.[2]

Of course making a move is something many people know how to do spontaneously. When they feel irritable or on the verge of losing their temper, they leave the house, saying they are going to 'take a walk' or 'get some air'. Others, if they have the means, will go travelling for a change of climate. Sometimes you only need to drink a glass of water or eat some fruit in order to change your inner state. But so many people prefer to reach for an aspirin or a glass of alcohol!

Of course there are events in life that plunge you into such turmoil and suffering that it is impossible to overcome them quickly. But so often you allow yourself to be troubled or overwhelmed by minor setbacks that could be so easily forgotten! Occasionally, you don't know why you feel sad or out of sorts, and in that case you must do everything you can to rid yourself of these states that affect your mood and behaviour. In such a situation, making a move can simply mean consciously washing your hands while concentrating on a word: light… harmony… beauty… love… and then passing your hands over your head and ears and washing them again. Do this several times if necessary. You will feel unburdened, for everything that was weighing you down will have left through the tips of your fingers.[3]

And if we must learn how to move, we must also know how to stay still. When you feel celestial currents moving through you, when you are visited by friends from the divine world, which can happen at any time, try to remain still for a few moments and allow yourself to be permeated by these currents and presences.

Now you understand how vast this question of place is, for it isn't limited to the social realm but embraces the whole of existence. As long as people haven't found their place, they are like seeds waiting to be sown. And their place is in fertile soil where they will be able to grow. So many people are still like seeds stored away in a granary! Until they are put in the earth they won't germinate, and their life will have no meaning for them. A seed that is planted in the earth germinates, grows, produces fruit and says, 'At last, I have found my place!' For its place was not in the granary where it would only shrivel or serve as food for the mice and worms; it was in the fertile soil of the spiritual world.

Once you have found the right place for your heart, your mind, your soul and your spirit, you will have found your true place. And then, wherever you are, whatever your material or social situation, you will feel at home. A symbol may help you to understand this. When treating other subjects I have often spoken to you of this symbol: a circle with a point in the centre.[4] The circle represents the vastness of infinite space, and the point in the centre is the spirit. The point is tiny, but thanks to the intensity of its vibrations it is present everywhere at once throughout the great expanse it sustains and vivifies. The solar system can be represented by this symbol and, at the other end of the scale, the cell as well. All creation is therefore present in this symbol.

You too must establish this structure within yourself: the circle with the point in the centre. You will only master your inner world by seeking to identify with your spirit, which is at the centre, as the only stable, immutable and indestructible reality. Concentrate on this central point: little by little you will feel yourself radiating outwards in all directions in space, and you will form a pure and powerful aura around yourself, which will attract the presence of heavenly entities.

Only those who have managed to form a circle of light around themselves have truly found their place. Thanks to this circle surrounding them, they benefit wherever they go from the best conditions for working and creating. Just as our physical body is protected by our skin, so our psychic body is protected by our aura. The moment we abandon this centre, it is as if this spiritual skin ruptures, and the slightest inconvenience causes us to lose our equilibrium and robs us of our peace. Only the centre, our spirit, is our true place.

Notes

1. See *'Et il me montra un fleuve d'eau de la vie',* part IV, chap. 1: 'La formation de l'univers et les différents âges de l'homme' and chap. 2: 'Les influences zodiacales sur nos six corps'; part XI, chap. 2: 'Les racines de la matière: les quatre Animaux saints'.
2. See *'Know Thyself' – Jnana Yoga,* Part 1, Complete Works, vol. 17, chap. 2: 'The synoptic table', and see above, Part 2, Complete Works, vol. 18, chap. 6: 'Concentration, meditation, contemplation and identification' and chap. 7: 'Prayer'.
3. See *The Mysteries of Fire and Water,* Izvor Coll. n° 232, chap. 15: 'Water, the universal medium'.
4. See *The Symbolic Language of Geometrical Figures,* Izvor Coll. n° 218, chap. 2: 'The circle'.

Chapter Seven

A COMMITMENT TO HEAVEN

Souls that have attained a certain degree of evolution sign a contract when they are about to incarnate on earth. They make a commitment in the presence of the entities of heaven to accomplish a mission, promising to develop their faculties and virtues in order to help and enlighten human beings. Whatever form this promise may take, it comes down to a promise to dedicate their qualities, their spiritual and material capabilities, to the service of others.

Nevertheless, since the incarnation of a soul is a progressive descent into matter during which it forgets what it has experienced above, by the time it reaches earth it is no longer fully conscious of the commitment it has made. But then gradually, it begins to feel certain sensations, impressions, thoughts and aspirations of a particular nature pass through it, vague and fleeting at first, but then increasingly precise. This manifests as a tendency to practise a certain activity, to contemplate a certain profession, which we call a vocation. This is why some people feel they must respond to a kind of calling, and why it is impossible for them not to respond in some way or other: they have the conviction that it is not only their own fulfilment and the meaning of their life that depend on this orientation but also the destiny of many other human beings.

Those who sense they have a mission to accomplish must not hesitate: since they have made a promise to the heavenly entities to sow certain seeds here below, to leave traces so others may benefit from their passage on earth, they are obliged to keep their commitment. These people may excel in different areas: philosophy, literature, science, spirituality, art or politics, but in each case they have a mission to fulfil for their fellow humans. Even if they don't explicitly tell themselves they are fulfilling a previously accepted mission, heaven arranges things so that they will feel in their element, in spite of any difficulties they may encounter on their route.

It is always possible, of course, that they will wander from their path and give in to certain temptations, until there is nothing left in them to remind them of the promises they made. Throughout history there have been great spirits, great initiates who have forgotten their mission and become lost on other paths. This is one of the difficulties of the spiritual life: remembering, at least vaguely, the promise made, doing everything possible to accomplish it, and knowing how to unmask the people and situations that may represent dangers, for all sorts of snares are placed on the path of the most evolved beings.

This is the meaning of the episode in the Gospels in which the devil comes to tempt Jesus by showing him all the rewards and satisfactions on earth.[1] This account is obviously symbolic. How could we believe such temptations were overcome during a brief conversation with the devil? This conversation represents the innumerable battles that even an initiate, even a great master must wage in order to expel all the dark entities that have taken hold within him, in his physical body and in his astral and mental bodies. Only on this condition can he truly fulfil his mission.

You may ask, 'But does this mean only certain souls descend to earth with a mission to fulfil? Do some of them incarnate without a particular purpose?' It is important to understand that all human beings are sons and daughters of God,[2] and that this imposes certain obligations on them. But not all souls have reached the same degree of evolution. Many are still weak and inexperienced, and they come down in order to learn and perfect themselves. For the time being, this is their only real duty, and they cannot be entrusted with great responsibilities. Signing a contract with heaven implies that you understand what you will have to face and are free to perform your task. But most souls are not free, and when they are obliged to descend to earth they aren't consulted about the family, society or country in which they would like to incarnate; destiny places them where they deserve to be, according to the law of justice.

Are you thinking this is a cruel way of treating souls and that God, who created them, should be more generous? Divine justice will respond that it has placed them where they need to be, and that if they had learned what they needed to learn in another incarnation they would have been treated differently.[3] Do parents consult a very young child about what they should do for him? No, they feed, wash and clothe him, they send him to school or take him on holidays without asking his opinion. They wait until he is older before consulting him and taking into account what he thinks and wants.

Very evolved souls have a certain freedom, which they have earned by their work over successive incarnations. This means that a soul can accept or refuse a mission proposed to it. It is asked, for example, 'In order to help such and such a people, do you agree to incarnate in this country, where you will have to live in difficult conditions and where great suffering awaits you?' And it is shown the conditions, which are often ones of poverty, hunger, violence and a lack of freedom, because this soul must share the same life conditions as everyone else. Even if the soul that accepts such an engagement is inwardly a prince or princess, it is not given privileged status.

So the soul thus consulted studies the situation, and, having seen the difficulties it will have to face, accepts or refuses. If it accepts, it becomes like an ambassador charged with a mission. It also happens that very capable men or women are offered certain positions of responsibility in a particular country which entail difficulties or even dangers. They are free to accept or not, whereas the ordinary civil servants are obliged to accept the position assigned to them, even if it is against their wishes.

When those who have accepted a mission allow themselves to become lost in the by-ways, they can only suffer, for they venture into regions where they cannot find what they aspire to in the depths of their being. You will say that others feel perfectly fine there… Yes, of course, because these regions correspond to their degree of evolution. But those who are destined to live and work in higher regions where they have everything they need to fulfil their task will face terrible suffering if they leave these regions.

Because they have already gained their freedom, those who are sent on a special mission are given extensive powers and have great means at their disposal. Of course they will encounter obstacles; they will be exposed to attacks, and they will suffer. But they are not left alone and without resources, for they are linked to the authorities they represent and receive information and support. A State doesn't send out ambassadors without putting lodging, funds and a qualified staff at their disposal. And since the suffering and difficulties these ambassadors of heaven encounter come from outside and not from themselves, they have forces in their soul and spirit that are immediately at their service when they call on them. This is not the case with most people: not that they are deprived of these inner resources – they do possess them – but they have allowed them to grow rusty.

And if you made promises to heaven before you incarnated on earth, you can rejoice. But don't simply rejoice, because it also entails great obligations. You have been given a great potential for work, but if you don't fulfil your mission, heaven will treat you severely. Of those who possess much, much is demanded.

Even if you cannot exactly remember that you have made a promise, it is always there within you in the form of noble aspirations and psychic tendencies. These are gifts you have been given, and failing to recognize that you have promised to use them for your own perfection and for the greater good is very serious. A strict accounting will be asked of you, yes, far stricter than of those who have promised nothing. Undoubtedly their life will also have difficulties and hardships, but these are adapted to the conditions their incarnation imposes on them. Whereas those who venture into regions foreign to the aspirations of their soul will suffer, all the more so if they pass abruptly from one extreme to another: when they are fulfilling their mission they experience profound joy, but as soon as they go astray they are thrown into the depths of despair.

While ordinary people are accustomed to the opaque atmosphere in which they live and transgress the laws without feeling troubled, those who have a high mission to fulfil no longer feel at peace when, however slightly, they transgress the laws of justice, love and disinterestedness. On the difficult terrain they travel, falls can be vertiginous, which is why they must increase their vigilance and take precautions. If the rewards awaiting them are great, the penalties for failure are terrible.

How do you know whether you are capable of keeping a promise you have made? Once you come to earth, you cannot know, but before descending, when this task was proposed to you, including the conditions in which you would have to accomplish it, all the elements were given to you so you could decide in full knowledge of the facts. You will never be asked for anything that is beyond your capabilities. A pupil taking an exam is asked questions corresponding to his or her level, not to a higher or lower one, and the questions are drawn from the current school year curriculum. In the same way, the celestial entities that propose a mission to you are aware of your capabilities and will not ask you to resolve problems or confront situations that are beyond you. But if you commit yourself, you must respect this commitment.

A promise is like a signature: it binds you until you achieve what you have promised. And not just to heaven: even promises you have made to human beings here below must be kept. If you leave this world without having had time to fulfil a commitment you have made, you must come back to do so. God himself is unable to release you from this promise: only the person to whom you have made it can do this. Some people are obliged to return to earth solely because of a broken promise from a previous incarnation. Nothing and no one is able to release them from it except, I repeat, the person to whom they have made it.

A man promises to marry a woman, and then one day he discovers he isn't made for marriage but for serving the Lord. Well, he must ask this woman to release him from this promise. It is not the Lord who can do it but this woman alone. If she refuses, it is useless for him to turn to the Lord, who will reply, 'Since you have promised, I can do nothing. I know you want to serve me, but you have plenty of time ahead of you. First go through with this marriage. You can also serve me as a married man.' How many sages, saints and prophets have had to come back to earth to acquit themselves of similar promises, made when they didn't yet know themselves well enough to discover their true vocation!

In order to get someone off your back, you may promise to do what the other asks, thinking, 'I can always promise, it doesn't commit me to anything!' Well, this is precisely where you are mistaken. Whoever the other person is, you must never make promises lightly, but know clearly what you are committing yourself to, for even if you are sincere at the moment, so many things can change with time! When someone asks something of me, I never promise but simply reply, 'I'll see what I can do,' because I know the magic power of a commitment: it binds us to each other forever.

The higher beings with whom we have signed a contract before descending to earth are watching to see that we fulfil it. So once we are here, we must try to recall what our soul has promised and execute it, without asking ourselves what it will cost in terms of effort, difficulties and fatigue. Nothing must stop us.

In my own case, I know what I promised… I had long surmised it, because it had taken such a strong hold in me that I couldn't ignore it. And when the Master Peter Deunov confirmed it, I no longer had the slightest doubt about it. In such a subtle domain as this, it is always possible to deceive oneself, so we must ask ourselves whether what we believe to be a vocation, a mission, hasn't simply arisen from an illusion about ourselves or an external influence… Once it is clear, however, we must no longer question ourselves but march resolutely forward.

Each of you must search deep within yourself to find the contract, the 'documents', which will perhaps show that you committed yourself to the celestial entities before coming to earth. In the silence and peace of deep meditation, search for these papers, these imprints. If after several attempts you find nothing, you need not be saddened. But don't be pleased either, saying to yourself, 'So much the better! I haven't made any promises, so I'm free to do what I like,' because by thinking this way you will never escape your limitations. This kind of freedom is an illusion, and everything you undertake in the name of such freedom can only tie you down. But human beings are strange: they rejoice in their weaknesses and boast about them as though they were great titles of honour, and they chase after their salvation in places where, in reality, their downfall awaits them.

You will know you are truly free the day heaven engages you for a high mission. Yes, for heaven doesn't engage creatures bound by selfish desires and destructive passions. It only engages beings who are free. But do people really want to be free? Some animals are so used to their cages that even if you open their door they don't leave: they have even lost their instinct for freedom. And unfortunately many human beings are just like them! They have forgotten that they too could live in freedom and don't even try to leave their prison. They could move beyond their limitations, but they don't dare, and some don't even think of it.

Whatever their present level of evolution, all human beings must strive to go further.[4] If they come up against insurmountable barriers, at least they will know their present limitations, which mustn't prevent them from wishing to surpass them eventually. On the other hand, if they encounter no obstacles, they will know they can continue along their path. Many people fail to advance because they imagine the road is closed. But perhaps it is open, and how will they know if they don't try to go forward? All human beings must experiment to find out what they are capable of. And even if they find they are unable to go very far, they need to know that the goal of their work is to attain the ideal that Jesus proposed to all of God's sons and daughters: *'Be perfect as your heavenly Father is perfect.'*[5]

Notes

1. See *'You are Gods'*, part II, chap. 3: 'The three great temptations'.
2. See *Sons and Daughters of God,* Izvor Coll. n° 240.
3. See *Truth: Fruit of Wisdom and Love,* Izvor Coll. n° 234, chap. 18: 'The truth will make you free'.
4. See *Youth: Creators of the Future,* Izvor Coll. n° 233.
5. See *The True Meaning of Christ's Teaching,* Izvor Coll. n° 215, chap. 3: 'Be perfect as your heavenly Father is perfect'.

Chapter Eight

FORGING AHEAD FEARLESSLY

On the long road of life, we make our way amidst all sorts of dangers, and we never know what may happen to us. So fear is a natural reaction. But this instinct, which is indispensable to the survival of the human race, can take forms that are completely irrational, so irrational that they have been the downfall of countless men and women instead of saving them. Many, overwhelmed by fear and panic, have thrown themselves into the fire, leapt into the void or drowned themselves!

And the causes of this fear are often just as irrational. People who are able to confront real dangers will flee from perfectly harmless spiders, mice or frogs. And there are those who would happily venture out at night in the mountains amid thunder and lightning but tremble at the idea of taking a plane or a lift. Why some fears and not others?

In Bulgaria, I had a friend who could hold her own in debate with any man. But when a fly or wasp began to fly around her in the street, she would run away screaming in panic, at the risk of being run over by a car. Several times I tried to reason with her, arguing that it was this fear that put her life in danger, not the flies and wasps, but to no avail. The only explanation for this kind of fear is that it is inscribed in the subconscious as a memory of accidents experienced in the near or distant past and, sometimes, even in a previous incarnation.

But whatever the causes and manifestations, the important thing is to learn to master fear. Since it paralyses thought and sweeps the body into chaotic reactions in the face of real or imaginary danger, you must first stop for at least a few seconds to keep from giving way to emotion and to gain control of yourself. Otherwise, you risk behaving like that passenger on an ocean liner that was about to sink: before being evacuated in a lifeboat, he wanted to go back to his cabin to retrieve his wallet with his papers. When he returned to the bridge, he was brandishing a roast chicken: in his panic he had gone to the kitchen instead!

In order to overcome fear, you mustn't give it the opportunity to trouble your spirit. Instead of trying to flee any way and anywhere you can, remain still for a few seconds and breathe deeply until you regain control over your heart, nervous system and limbs. If you allow your limbs to become agitated, you lose complete control of them. It is as if you had opened the door of a cage of wild animals: once they have escaped, it is very difficult to get them back in. On the other hand, if you introduce other reflexes in place of this agitation, you will become calmer; everything will return to order, and you will be able to make the best decisions.

What makes fear especially difficult to master is the abrupt nature of the events that provoke it: people suddenly find themselves in a situation that is not only worrisome but unexpected. During the Second World War, there was a battery of canons that fired every night near our house at Sèvres, so we were constantly awakened with a start. I explained to my friends that before going to sleep they should fix the idea firmly in their minds that at some time during the night they would be awoken by bombardments. By doing so they would overcome their fear and endure the inevitable shock to their nervous system less painfully. You must always call on your conscious will for help; otherwise, you risk giving way, out of panic, to actions that are more dangerous than the danger itself. I have experienced this myself.

At times during the war,* I had to go to Paris, and when I returned to Sèvres by train I was sometimes caught under fire as I left the station. Believe me when I tell you that I walked calmly, without feeling the slightest fear. But one day as I left the station I started to run in order to avoid the shrapnel that was falling from all directions, until I suddenly realized that hurrying in this way had activated an instinctive fear in me that was steadily building. Unhappy with this observation, I stopped dead in my tracks. I called on my willpower for help in regaining my calm, and I succeeded, but with difficulty. This experience

*The second World War.

taught me what I am explaining to you today. By running I had triggered the fear that lies deep in every human being. The people we call courageous are not those who feel no fear but those who have learned to master it.

We don't often hear fear mentioned as one of the human weaknesses, and yet it is a great enemy of inner progress. Behind cowardice, greed, malice and aggression, often there is fear. You meet people who claim to be afraid of nothing, but what do they mean by that? In fact, if they really knew how to analyse themselves, they would notice there is at least one thing or one person they are afraid of. Everything that exists in the visible and invisible worlds can serve as an object of apprehension, and I won't enumerate all the different forms of fear: they are infinite, from the fear of accidents, illness and death to that of public opinion, lack of money, a husband's or wife's infidelity, and so on. Fear accompanies men and women throughout their lives and clouds their inner sky. So we must be prepared to confront it at any moment.

When we analyse the causes of fear, we realize that it is founded above all on the feeling that we are at risk of losing something or someone. People sometimes wonder where the serene facial expression, characteristic of certain sages, comes from. Well, it comes quite simply from the fact that they have managed to overcome their fear of losing anything whatsoever. They have risen to this summit where they sense that something indestructible exists within them, something that can never be taken from them.[1] Whatever happens to them, true sages know that the only reality, both in themselves and in all beings, is this summit that is sheltered from all adversity: the spirit, the spark that God has transmitted to all human creatures. This is why sages feel no fear, either for themselves or for others.

But how do you reach this point? By working on yourself, by purifying your thoughts and feelings and thereby gradually dissolving the opaque layers that separate you from this divine spark and prevent you from sensing it as the only reality. What religion calls 'providence' is this certitude, deeply held by certain beings who have experienced it, that something within them is absolutely beyond all attack and eludes all vicissitudes.

Dangers exist, and I don't advise you to confront them unnecessarily or to avoid taking precautions simply because I have given you methods for overcoming fear. For your fearlessness will not necessarily prevent you from becoming a victim. You may not be afraid of burglars, but close your doors and windows securely when you leave your house, and don't go venturing into just any old place either. I am simply trying to put you on your guard against the uncontrollable reactions you could experience when faced with something or someone that frightens you. I repeat, at such times do not move or speak; link yourself with the Divinity that dwells within you, and ask to be shown how to conduct yourself. But understand that your success in receiving responses from the Divinity will depend on the extent to which you have cleared a path to it.[2]

This is why it is important not to wait until you are faced with great dangers before practising. Every day you have occasion to find yourself suddenly confronted with facts or situations that can arouse fear in you, even if it is merely words... For example, someone threatens to deprive you of something important to you or to block one of your worthy projects. Instead of instantly feeling afraid and reacting in an aggressive way, leaving and slamming the door behind you, keep quiet and stay calm, because if you react impulsively it will only make matters worse. Who is to say these aren't merely idle threats? And if they are real, you will deal with them more successfully if you know how to stay level-headed. Try to call to mind all the occasions when you reacted impulsively, out of fear of what you considered a danger, and later regretted it.

Some people are daring and count on inspiring fear in others to help them realize their projects. That is why the audacious appreciate cowards so much; they will certainly be of no help to them in their shady schemes, but at least they don't bother them but cautiously step aside and let them pass. Heaven itself doesn't appreciate cowards, because they are like leaky jugs that hold nothing: faced with problems or obstacles, they forget everything they believe in and are capable of the utmost cowardice. Heaven seeks bold, intrepid beings, beings who, once they have encountered the light, face up to all the obstacles that can arise within or without.

Try, then, to overcome fear in all its forms. You will say it is written in the book of Proverbs, *'The fear of the Lord is the beginning of wisdom'*. Yes, but this fear isn't exactly the same as the kind I have been talking about; we have to make a distinction. The fear I have been talking about is an instinct that arises from the dark depths of the subconscious and, as we have seen, often has no basis in fact. The second kind of fear has a mental nuance: when we fear something or someone in this way, we know why.

In Proverbs, it isn't this instinctive fear but fear of the Lord that is said to be the beginning of wisdom. There is no need to fear the Lord instinctively; he wishes us no ill, on the contrary. But we must be afraid of breaking his laws. This fear, then, comes from understanding that the universe created by God obeys certain laws and that the transgression of these laws can only harm us, because it puts us at odds with the cosmic order.

Darkness can be a cause of irrational fear: you imagine that a wolf, a thief or a mugger is going to jump out at you! But it can also be the cause of a rational fear: when you can't see anything, you are always at risk of bumping into something, or falling and hurting yourself. The wiser and more intelligent people grow, the more they become not exactly fearful in the sense we generally understand this word but prudent and watchful. And at the same time they become more audacious, intellectually, mentally.

They are wary of what comes from their feelings and instincts, which can cloud their view, but in relation to what is clear and limpid they become audacious. This is why people who are truly intelligent and knowledgeable are bolder than others. They venture into regions most people never dare to approach, and it is the light that gives them this boldness.

The wiser and more enlightened you are, the more conscious you become of dangers and try not to provoke them, but at the same time you become bold, because you know you can trust what you know. Throughout life, human beings never lose their sense of danger, but this feeling evolves until it is only the fear of transgressing the divine order, of becoming a false note in the cosmic harmony. You may say that human beings aren't important enough to destroy the cosmic harmony. Well, this is where you are wrong: it only takes a selfish action, a pointless or malicious word.[3]

But it is also not advisable to be constantly on edge, with the idea that every word, every action, every thought or feeling may be a false note. Such fear is paralysing: if you imagine that with every step you could be guilty of making a mistake, you won't progress.

This fear that paralyses human beings has been used by certain religions to further their own ends. In the Middle Ages, for example, the Church was constantly preaching to Christians about the punishments of hell. It claimed to be acting for the good of their souls, but in reality this method did great damage. You could even say that souls became havens for the devil, for in thinking so much about him, people forgot about God. Any number of portraits of the devil were made! He was drawn, sculpted and painted, and in their spoken and written sermons, preachers made excessive use of him. They used him the same way people threaten children with the police, the wolf or the bogeyman.

I'm talking about the Middle Ages, but I'm not sure whether in our day and age there aren't people who still use religion in such a way. All of this is very negative from the pedagogical point of view. Contrary to what they hypocritically profess, those who act in this way have no concern at all for the good of people's souls but are merely trying to exercise their power over them. And if they are sincere, it isn't much better: it means they are ill!

It is true that real evolution is an ongoing ascent. But during this ascent every human being inevitably passes through highs and lows, ups and downs, and it is important to know this if you are to maintain your courage and persevere. One day there will be more ups than downs, and because God is a loving father he forgives those of his children who recognize their mistakes and decide to correct them.

It is impossible to grow spiritually without ever experiencing failure. What is important is that you have taken the path towards the heights, the path of love and wisdom that leads to truth.[4] That you will occasionally fall or take a few steps backwards along this path is not so serious. What is important is that you maintain the same direction, that you keep this same goal, this same ideal alive in you, that you keep your eyes fixed on the summit to be attained.

The only thing to fear is deviating from your path and losing the awareness that you are sons and daughters of God, who are awaited in the house of the Father.[5] Yes, this fear alone is allowed, and even recommended, for it is this fear that will gradually deliver you from all the fears that limit and weaken you, enabling you to advance along the path with assurance, peace and clarity.

Notes

1. See *'In Spirit and in Truth',* Izvor Coll. n° 235, chap. 4: 'Reaching for the top' and chap. 5: 'From multiplicity to unity'.
2. See *'Et il me montra un fleuve d'eau de la vie',* part X, chap. 1: 'La porte du monde psychique: Iésod'.
3. See *Harmony and Health,* Izvor Coll. n° 225, chap. 2: 'The world of harmony'.
4. See *Truth: Fruit of Wisdom and Love,* Izvor Coll. n° 234.
5. See *'You are Gods',* part 1, chap. 3: 'The return to the house of the Father'.

Chapter Nine

THE LIGHT OF THE SPIRIT SHOULD BE OUR ONLY GUIDE

How many men and women feel like kings and queens in exile, divested of their throne! They are conscious of a worthiness which they think no one acknowledges in them, and they suffer from the conditions they have been given in life. Their society has no regard for them and even makes them feel useless. But what is society? A vast theatrical stage where all sorts of comedies are played out. So why should these comedies make them forget that what matters is what they are in themselves, not the spectacle they present on this stage? If only they would keep their faith in the immensity of their soul and the power and light of their spirit. Do they really need the respect of others? And even if they become the object of such respect, don't they know how fickle public opinion is?

Look at what happens with celebrities. One day the eyes of the whole world are fixed on them, and a little while later they are forgotten. One day they are praised to the skies, and the next they are assassinated. Sometimes the two even happen at the same time: while they are being admired and glorified by some people, others are tearing them to pieces. How will they end up, then, if they don't know how to cling to something stable and solid within themselves: to their spirit?

There is an interesting little anecdote about the great tenor Caruso. One year, having sung the principal roles in several operas at the Metropolitan Opera in New York, he was celebrated as a triumphant success. Everyone told him, 'People everywhere will recognize you by your voice, it is unique!' Caruso was very flattered, of course, but wanted to see whether it was true. So one day when he was to sing at La Scala in Milan, he arranged to replace a tenor who was singing a secondary role. Of course no one knew about it, and this is what happened: unaware that it was Caruso who had come onto the stage, the public hardly reacted. Then, as soon as he entered to play the principal role, there was thunderous applause before he had even opened his mouth. Obviously, this caused him to reflect. Often the public is only responding to someone's name and reputation… until they get carried away by someone else!

The Creator has made all of us stewards of gifts, of faculties and talents, which we must cultivate to the greatest extent possible. You will say this is a great deal of work and effort, which others may not recognize… But why is it so important to you that your talents are recognized? God gave you these riches, and he sees what you make of them. It isn't reasonable that the efforts you make to perfect yourself depend on the opinion of others; the only opinion that counts is the Creator's.

For those who are unhappy about remaining behind the scenes, success and fame appear to be advantageous. But if they were to talk to those who have these advantages, they would hear about all the inconveniences they entail… For different reasons, of course, it isn't so easy to find the right attitude towards either success or failure, so the only solution is to attach little importance to either one.

What is essential is that we learn to use our faculties to deepen our connection with our heavenly Father. If others recognize our faculties and benefit from them, so much the better, but that is a different matter and not one that should preoccupy us. Our task is to develop ourselves in a balanced and harmonious way, so that we draw closer and closer to the image of the Creator which we carry imprinted within us. Because in reality, those intellectual or artistic gifts that don't help us to rediscover this divine imprint do not necessarily make us happy.[1]

How many scientists, philosophers, writers, poets and artists live in torment! And while the public is enriched by their works, they themselves would willingly exchange their immense talent for a few days of inner peace. You ask, 'But why is there so much disorder and tragedy in the lives of such remarkable people?' Because they are content to cultivate the gift they have received from heaven, without bothering to work deeply at improving their way of life. Many of them even think it is their passions, torments and lack of balance that nurture their talent, and in a certain sense they foster them.

It is true that there are exceptional people, whose achievements in art and thought, as well as in the spiritual realm, are most often born of the sufferings and profound difficulties they have somehow been able to overcome. But if such difficulties are truly to be surmounted, an inner spiritual work is required, and if this work is non-existent or insufficient, it will eventually lead to psychic imbalance, with all the anguish and suffering that come with it. In order to endure these, some turn to drink, drugs or debauchery. Since they possess real gifts, this doesn't prevent them from creating masterpieces from time to time. But it is others who benefit from their works, not they themselves. They suffer, and they continue to suffer until they finally discipline themselves and master the dark forces that are gradually destroying them.

But this is a subject most people don't think about. For them, it is enough that certain books or works of art interest and inspire them; they are not much concerned with what has become of the author. The fact that many of them come to a tragic end, that they sink into madness or commit suicide, is considered almost normal, and people eagerly pounce on the biographies of these extraordinary beings to revel in the slightest details. There is great cruelty in this fascination on the public's part, but most people are obviously unaware of it.

And above all, what these artists don't realize is that those who refuse to nurture their gifts and faculties through inner discipline will lose them sooner or later, either during this life or the next. Since they have squandered all their capital through a dissolute life, they will return to earth as completely insignificant beings. Our moral life cannot be separated from our artistic or intellectual life for long.[2]

We have seen outstanding artists living in debauchery and perversion, and many in their circle wonder how they are capable of expressing heaven while living in hell. They themselves don't know. They are unaware that luminous spirits of the invisible world come to manifest in them in the hope of saving them. Yes, this mysterious talent that reveals itself in certain people is a sort of bridge, which spiritual entities establish between them and heaven. These entities write, paint, compose, sing and play through the beings they inhabit, making immense sacrifices in an attempt to release them from hell. If these artists persist on the path of self-destruction, these spirits eventually abandon them; they do so with sadness, but they have no alternative. And even if they were once considered geniuses, these poets, painters, musicians and philosophers find themselves naked and poor, deprived of their talents.

If you really need the understanding and appreciation of others, take care in choosing those people whose respect you hope to have. What does honey gain from being appreciated by wasps, the lamb by the wolf or the rich man by thieves? You will say you know all that. But are you really sure? Are you sure that in order to attract the approval or applause of others, you do nothing that goes against justice, wisdom, kindness, generosity and beauty?

What are you doing when you join in with people who are criticizing or mocking someone? Deep down you know that this criticism or ridicule is often exaggerated, but in order to please others or show how witty you are, you add your two cents' worth. And in the artistic or even the political domain, how many people compromise their integrity in order to succeed! They never try to gain the appreciation of sages and initiates; there is no advantage in that, because there are so few of them! They would only have a meagre audience or very few votes in an election.

Artists, both men and women, have come to the Brotherhood and shown me their works. Some of them create abstract paintings or 'concrete music'. And when I ask in astonishment whether this combination of strokes and spots or these sequences of discordant sounds really mean something to them, they reply that traditional concepts of art are out of date today, and that in order to attract the attention of art or music lovers you have to explore new paths. That may be true, but where do such paths lead?

A music hall performer even explained to me that, having grown tired of making people laugh with trivial jokes, hc had written a theatrical piece inspired by mysticism, because deep down he felt he was a mystic. But this piece had been a failure: the public had understood nothing of his intentions, and he had been forced to return to his former routines. Of course it is difficult to appeal to the public with spiritual subjects, and all the more so if you haven't worked deeply and at length on these subjects until you are able to express what will touch your audience in the most profound part of themselves. How can anyone believe it's possible to go from bawdy comedy to spirituality overnight?[3]

There is nothing more precious than having a quality, a gift, a faculty that is capable of awakening the divine in people. But it is also necessary to be conscious of it and decide to consecrate such a gift to this end. How many women who are aware of their beauty ask themselves what effect this beauty is having on others? Whether it is beauty, or artistic or intellectual faculties, strive to use them only to awaken this divine spark, this sacred flower that slumbers within all beings. In doing so you will attract the joys of heaven to yourself.

We have not come to earth to gain applause at any price. Whatever we do, we must be guided by the light of the spirit and gain the approval of heaven. If human beings also appreciate us, all well and good, but our conduct should never be determined by their opinion. In any case, there is always someone who appreciates and understands you: the One who created you. He knows very well what you are worth. He knows he has placed within you a spark of immortal life, your spirit, and this is all you need.

Even if your material means are limited, even if there isn't much of a place for you in society and you don't find the right conditions for acting and making a mark for yourself with your abilities, that is no reason to feel inferior, rejected or useless. In fact, you can become extraordinarily and uniquely valuable by working for the coming of the kingdom of God and his righteousness on earth.[4] When you imbue every thought, feeling and action with the idea of the kingdom of God, you will feel something developing in you that nothing and no one can take from you.

And in the meantime, many of those who occupied the limelight fade and disappear. Deprived of those activities that attracted others' attention, they sink into idleness. And how they suffer when they realize that what they poured all their energies into building up for so many years could be destroyed overnight by their successors! Whereas those who work in the background for the kingdom of God feel something growing within them that no human regard, no human glory can ever eclipse or even equal.

The worst situation in life is to feel useless. Many people wander about aimlessly, claiming they are incapable of making any kind of a name for themselves in society; from sheer boredom they yawn and scratch themselves where they don't even itch! To the point where some, who are incapable of finding any useful outlet for their energies, even end up committing crimes. It isn't because their nature is particularly bad, but because they feel ignored and despised and can only express themselves through violence or delinquency. Then, of course, they are finally noticed.

To be sensitive to the regard and opinion of others isn't reprehensible in itself. Your self-respect, your sense of your own worth, however, must never depend on this regard, this opinion, but on your awareness of the work you can accomplish in the secret of your heart when you allow yourself to be guided by the light of the spirit. Perhaps you feel society doesn't acknowledge you or need you? This shouldn't upset you: you will always find a way and a place to work for the coming of the kingdom of God and his righteousness. Thanks to this consciousness of doing something useful, everything good and beautiful in you will awaken, be nourished and grow, and you will be astonished to experience so many new feelings of peace, expansiveness, freedom and true joy.

Perhaps you would like a king to appoint you his minister? Well, why not? But this depends on all sorts of external circumstances, so if you persist with this ambition you risk exhausting yourself to no avail. On the other hand, putting yourself in the service of the King of Heaven depends on you alone, and in this you can aim very high.

In your inner life, your spiritual life, you must aspire to a place at the King's side, but in worldly affairs it is best not to set our sights so high. If you are really needed you will eventually be found, but it doesn't mean you will be very happy when you find yourself overburdened by responsibilities and worries. Initiates never seek high positions in society, but in their inner life they aim at positions so high you can't even see them. Like them, ask for a great deal inwardly, and accept a modest place in society if your destiny doesn't offer you something more glorious. There are always enough candidates to fill the positions of general, minister, president or director…

Avoid involving yourself in exhausting struggles. Choose to go where you have the most space, or perhaps even where you can be alone, for there no one will try to hinder your growth. If you plant yourself by the side of a great, fast-growing tree, it will protest and cry out for the space vital to it. Don't wander into the territory of a wild animal either. Instead, be like a bird. What chance would a bird have if it decided to compete for space with a wild animal, with its tiny body, so weak and delicate, and its little beak? But it also has wings and can fly freely in the sky. A bird has no ambition to impose itself upon a wild animal. It thanks the Creator every day for giving it song and its freedom of movement.

True sons and daughters of God are like birds. They don't want to cut a path through the jungle. Instead, guided by the light of the spirit, they seek to fly heavenward each day and to bring back peace, light and joy, which they will share with all their brothers and sisters.[5]

Notes

1. See *'You are Gods'*, part III: 'So God created humankind in his image'.
2. See *'Et il me montra un fleuve d'eau de la vie'*, part VII, chap. 1: 'Le talent ne suffit pas'.
3. See *Creation: Artistic and Spiritual,* Izvor Coll. n° 223, chap. 2: 'The divine sources of inspiration'.
4. See *A New Dawn: Society and Politics in the Light of Initiatic Science,* Complete Works, vol. 26, chap. 5: 'The kingdom of God and his righteousness'.
5. See *Sons and Daughters of God,* Izvor Coll. n° 240, chap. 13: 'Sons and daughters of God are brothers and sisters to all people'.

Chapter Ten

OUR PLACE ON THE COSMIC TREE

Increasingly, over the centuries, humans have succeeded in dominating nature. They actually believe this is their role in the world, and they call it progress, culture, civilization. In fact, now that they have disrupted climates, polluted the earth, the sky and the oceans and devastated the flora and fauna, they feel they can proudly claim the title of cultivated, civilized creatures!

Of course, nature is patient, very patient. But when it senses that humans are persisting in disturbing the order that governs it, it retaliates, and they must suffer the effects of this retaliation not only in their surroundings but in themselves. They believe they are free to engage in all kinds of abuses with impunity, without foreseeing that the same disorder they create in nature they also create in their physical body and psyche. And if they cannot get along with each other, this too is because they have failed to respect the order the Creator has established in nature and in themselves.[1]

Those who have learned to harmonize with the order established by the Creator don't impose themselves on nature, nor do they impose themselves on other human beings. They don't oppress them or try to use them to their own advantage. And above all, by their conduct and their mastery over their inner world, they do their best to contribute to the development and freedom of others.

On the physical plane, human beings are individual and separate, and each person's experiences do not directly affect others. Your suffering or your joy does not appear to be their suffering or their joy. If you persist in eating indigestible food, you will damage your own stomach, not theirs. But on high, in the subtle planes, there are no barriers, and all your inner states produce effects on some creature or another. Yes, because on high only one creature exists: cosmic Man, who is the synthesis of all creatures. We live in this cosmic Man, in fact we are this cosmic Man, and no creature exists in him as a separate entity. There is a moral law, therefore, that follows from this: you can do neither good nor evil to others without doing the same good or evil to yourself. On the face of it, this doesn't make much sense: if you kick someone who is annoying you, it is he or she who feels the pain, whereas you are relieved, or at least you think you are. But in actual fact, this law makes a great deal of sense, for within the cosmic Man, we are all one.

One of the most significant symbols of this cosmic Man is the tree. A tree sinks it roots deep into the earth while it sends its branches out in all directions in space. Suppose each root considered itself an individual, isolated from the others: it wouldn't notice that higher up it is linked to a trunk which divides into branches, and that on these branches there are flowers and fruits.

So it could be said that we humans represent the roots, buried in the earth, of one tree. Every day we absorb elements from the earth with which to nourish the trunk and branches of this tree that is humanity. And humanity in turn represents a root of the cosmic Tree, on which each human being is like a rootlet. Yes, the whole of humanity is comparable to a root, and each rootlet feeds on, breathes in and draws from the earth forces, which then rise all the way up the trunk.

In this reservoir that is matter, every human being draws in raw elements, which he or she transforms and sends into the great root that is humanity. But before reaching the great root, there are several stages these elements must pass through: the sap collected by the rootlets nourishes a small root, the family, which nourishes a bigger root, the country; the country nourishes the continent, and finally the sap reaches the great root, which is humanity. This passage from individual to humanity takes place via roots that are progressively larger and linked to each other. As for the tree, it soars upward from the ground, rising ever higher into the air and light.

But is this earth, with the life it sustains, the only one in the cosmos? No, on the moon, on Mercury, on Venus, Mars, Jupiter, Saturn and others there are of course other 'humanities' (we will call them that, even though we are talking about creatures very different from ourselves). They represent other roots, and these converge to create a root that unites with yet other roots, with other families of beings in the solar system and even far beyond in the galaxies and nebulas. It is this entire ensemble that represents the cosmic Tree, God himself, of which the sephirotic tree of the cabbalists is one representation.[2] From the roots of the sephirotic tree (*Malkuth,* the kingdom), currents of energy rise all the way to the summit, to *Kether,* the crown. *(See p 110)*

Because life circulates from the tips of the roots to the tips of the branches as well as the other way round, the cosmic Tree is undoubtedly the best representation of the unity of creation. But initiates have also expressed this unity with the symbol of the serpent biting its own tail. The head corresponds to the world of the spirit, and the tail to that of matter. Spirit and matter are the two aspects of God that manifest and act throughout the whole of his creation. Nothing we see is separate from God. He represents the totality, and we exist somewhere within him as cells of his immense body. And since we too are matter and spirit, our task is to continually nourish our spirit by drawing on our matter and to breathe into our matter the eternally renewed life of the spirit.[3]

Through a multitude of ramifications, we belong to the cosmic Being; we are identical to this cosmic Being. That is why, although on the physical plane we

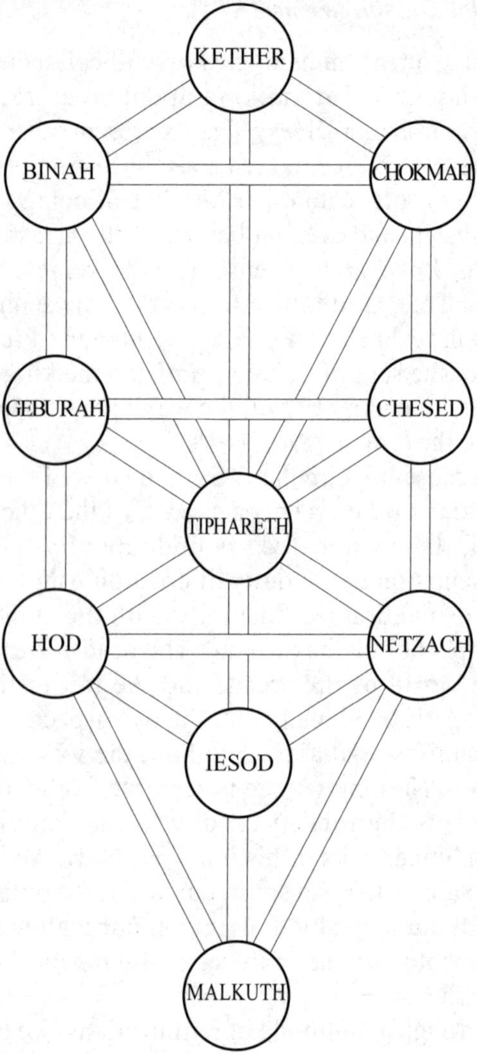
KETHER
BINAH
CHOKMAH
GEBURAH
CHESED
TIPHARETH
HOD
NETZACH
IESOD
MALKUTH

COSMIC TREE

may believe we are separate from others, in the subtle regions we are connected, and we can do neither good nor ill to others without doing it to ourselves as well. When you have become imbued with this idea, you will understand that before you can do good to others, you must begin by doing good to yourself.

If you work with your thoughts, your feelings and your actions to build something good within yourself, it will become so deeply embedded in you that you will no longer be capable of doing harm. Strive to be attentive to yourself. What a magnificent apprenticeship! In this way you will become attentive to others as well. In the true science, you start with yourself, not your little egotistic self, but your higher self, your cosmic Self.

And what does it mean to 'start with yourself'? You can speak to the entities that dwell within you, for example. Instead of giving free rein to your lower nature by constantly complaining and becoming indignant over everything and nothing, learn to argue a little with all those creatures in you who are worried, disgruntled and rebellious – yes, those beings you have been carrying around with you for incarnations and who have finally become embedded in you in the form of bad habits. You must persuade them to be quiet. And at the same time, call upon your higher nature to manifest through all the wise and enlightened entities who also inhabit you. Let them speak, and accept their good suggestions; they will be useful to you, both for yourself and for others.[4]

So many people claim they want to be useful, to do good in the world around them! But good thoughts and good intentions aren't enough. People who want to help others must become conductors of the divine life, and for that they must rid themselves of everything that can attract dark forces. Good and evil are so intimately entangled within all human beings that dark forces often manage to take advantage of their good intentions. And when they decide to do good, all sorts of elements foreign to this good get mixed up in their actions.

By working patiently every hour of every day, you must try to diminish those states that serve as magnets to negative forces and, on the other hand, try to intensify those states that attract heavenly currents to you. When you have nothing left that can open the door to evil, then, yes, you will become true conductors of divine light.

To help you in this work, you can even make use of certain objects. As I have already explained, the universe forms an immense unity in which everything is connected. 'That which is below is like that which is above, and that which is above is like that which is below', says Hermes Trismegistus. Therefore, every material object corresponds to something on the subtle planes, particularly on the astral plane. Sorcerers and black magicians base their activity on this law: they link a physical object to a corresponding current of forces, the object serving as a medium for the mobilization of these forces. With the aid of a poison, for example, over which they pronounce incantations and carry out a special ritual, they manage to stir up the lower levels of the astral plane, and they project the harmful influence of this poison onto the person they have in mind, who actually becomes poisoned.

This happens because the sorcerer, by applying the law of correspondences, establishes a link between the physical and psychic planes, so that the physical poison can act on the astral poison of hatred, jealousy and vengeance and insinuate itself into people. There are so many books describing these practices of black magic, and I ask you never to resort to them. There are many fewer works presenting the practices of white magic. And why are there so few of them, when this same law also applies to the realm of the good?[5]

Understand that, in fact, an object that has harmonious lines and beautiful colours and is made of beautiful material corresponds on the subtle planes to something beneficial and vivifying. You can use it to stir up the higher layers of the astral planes, thanks to the forces represented by the divine virtues. As you concentrate on the virtues of love, wisdom, truth, goodness, justice, purity, peace and sacrifice, reinforcing them within you, this object allows you to contact beneficial forces, which will pour forth over people.

Here is an activity for the disciples of an initiatic teaching who have delved into the mysteries of the cosmic Tree: work with the antidotes to evil, learn to use objects and symbols in order to link them to their corresponding virtues on high. Once set in motion, these forces are able to cleanse, detoxify, organize and vivify everything.

But where are there people who are conscious of these spiritual realities and determined to help themselves in order to help the whole world? Never forget that everything you do to yourself and for yourself, good or bad, reflects on others. This is a law, and nothing is more important than to know the laws governing nature and our inner world, so we may participate in a work that is truly beneficial for all of humanity.

Notes

1. See *'Cherchez le Royaume de Dieu et sa Justice',* part VII, chap. 4: 'L'homme dans le corps cosmique'.
2. See *Angels and other Mysteries of the Tree of Life,* Izvor Coll. n° 236, chap. 1: 'From man to God: the notion of hierarchy', chap. 2: 'Introduction to the sephirotic Tree of Life' and chap. 11: 'The body of Adam Kadmon'.
3. See *The Philosopher's Stone – in the Gospels and in Alchemy,* Izvor Coll. n° 241, chap. 3: 'You are the salt of the earth'.
4. See *The Path of Silence,* Izvor Coll. n° 229, chap. 6: 'The inhabitants of silence' and chap. 7: 'Harmony, the essential condition for inner silence'.
5. See *The Book of Divine Magic,* Izvor Coll. n° 226.

Chapter Eleven

'GOING ABROAD'

We so often hear how selfish and insensitive people are to the suffering and misfortune of others! And yet there are so many who show spontaneous compassion for this suffering and misfortune and who are determined to help. They swing into action: they talk, they intervene, they launch initiatives. There is absolutely no doubt in their minds: once they decide they sincerely want to help others, they can do so. They are unaware that to do good is a whole science in itself and that merely wanting to be useful to our family, friends or society doesn't actually make us capable of being so.

Suppose you are walking along a river and you see someone drowning. Listening only to your good-heartedness, you jump into the water. But unless you are aware of the desperate energy that takes hold of people when they are drowning, you will let this person grab onto your arms and will go down with him or her. You must never allow someone who is drowning to grab your arms. You must make them hold onto your waist, for example, and if need be even stun them a little with a blow. They will consider you cruel at the time perhaps, but that doesn't matter, since it is the only way you can both be saved. Later on they will recognize that you were wise to act as you did.

Perhaps you will say you already know this. Yes, but it is a question of how you interpret this image. This same situation can confront us in life in different forms, but whatever the circumstances, you must always maintain the freedom of your 'limbs', or you will go down with those you want to help. So many people have been victims of their good intentions! After such an experience, they close themselves off and for the rest of their lives regret even having tried to help others. You should never stop wanting to do good, but only on condition that you know how: which means, by keeping your limbs, or more precisely your arms, free, by maintaining your freedom of action.

In many poor countries, the men decide to go abroad to earn money and provide for the needs of their family. It looks as if they are abandoning their wife and children, but in fact it is completely the opposite: it is precisely because they are thinking of their family that they go away. In other words, they don't allow their family to paralyse their arms, for this is the only way they are able to save them from suffering. You will say, 'But how does this example concern us?' It concerns you because you live in a world where, even if you don't have to rescue your family from physical misery, you constantly meet men and women who are anxious and unhappy.

What means do you have to help them? You say you will share their grief, you will suffer with them… But even if they are touched to see that you aren't indifferent to their misfortunes, what does your compassion really do for them?

You can only help others if you make a daily habit of visiting a country abounding in riches, which is to say, in love, light and joy. This country is the divine world.[1] How can people who are poor, anxious and joyless offer any support to others? Draw closer to God; this is where you will find all nourishment and all forces for your heart and soul. And then, not only will you be able to distribute them to those around you but by your example you will teach others to do the same. Once you have achieved certain realizations on the psychic plane, it is easier to obtain them on the physical plane.

Many people imagine that prayer, meditation and action are incompatible. Well, this is the greatest error! Many men and women of action were true mystics. Of course there were also many who were not, but exactly what good did they do? People who immediately rush into action without first seeking light from the Spirit run the risk of causing nothing but disorder and destruction. An action is only beneficial if it is well directed. And how can it be well directed if certain conditions are not fulfilled? What can you do without resources and, above all, without inner light?

Those who truly want to help others must learn how to leave them behind in order to rise to God.

Even the best people with the best intentions will not do much good if they rely only on their own capabilities, their own inspiration. You have to possess great spiritual wealth if you want to be useful. The pauper contributes nothing.

Under the pretext that they love them, people remain physically close to others in order to care for them. But how can they help them if they don't rid themselves of their own limitations, their own weaknesses and mediocrity? This kind of love is not enough. We see it clearly in the realm of education. Just because parents are busy looking after their children, it doesn't mean they are educating them. To truly educate them, they must be able to offer them something else, something luminous and solid from above that will remain with their children throughout their lives. You cannot educate children simply by telling them, 'Eat, sleep, wrap up well, look before you cross the road, do your best at school, choose your friends carefully, don't smoke, don't drink alcohol, don't take drugs…' This advice, these instructions and rules are certainly useful, but they don't nourish a child's soul and spirit. And parents should be under no illusions: if they fail to nourish their children's soul and spirit, they are not protecting them.[2]

So if you want to help others, begin by leaving them and forgetting about them for at least a few minutes! You will only appear to have forgotten them, for in fact you will be able to think of much better ways to help them than if you had stayed by their side. I myself have understood that if I remain here with you all the time, I cannot help you. So I leave you from time to time to rise to God, where I collect riches, which I can then share with you. I don't rely much on my presence among you. You have had this often enough and haven't necessarily benefited a great deal from it.

So you must make a habit of leaving your wife, your husband, your children or your friends in order to travel abroad (to the divine world), to collect peace and light, and then return to distribute it to them. A weak and poor man can only transmit his own troubles and distress, and sometimes, even when he puts his whole heart into it, he only makes things worse. The only way to help others, to save them, is to return on high each day to the celestial homeland we have temporarily left and to collect gifts there, which we will bring back to them. Otherwise, what form will our help take?

You have certainly had this kind of experience yourself. Yes, aren't there people you prefer never to talk to about your difficulties, because you know that, under the pretext of helping, they will only complicate everything? Well, if you don't want to be one of those people whom others avoid confiding in for fear of attracting new problems, you need to reflect, meditate and pray in order to find the best ways of helping others.

Of course, someone who is unhappy may feel relieved at the thought that they are not alone in their suffering, but to tell someone who is in tears that you understand, that you share their sadness, is not enough to truly help them. Instead of adopting the same long face, you should do the opposite and nourish such great faith and so much joy in yourself that these neutralize their pain. And if their suffering is expressed through anger, you must on no account share in this anger, but remain calm.

Where did I learn this method? From Master Peter Deunov. I didn't understand the reasons for his attitude toward other people's suffering until later on. Initiates and sages do not behave in the same way as those who are ignorant.

If you want to help others, don't be receptive to their negative states. When someone is upset, you won't make this person any better by entering into the same state of anguish. You must withdraw somewhere, gather your joy, and then return and shower him or her with this joy. What have you learned in the teaching of the Universal White Brotherhood if you still don't know how to help others? You say you love them, but it isn't true. If you loved them you would give thanks to heaven and earth; you would lift your heart and mind to God, saying, 'Lord, I love them, give me something for them.'

This is how you can be useful. Those who try to help others with their own resources fail to obtain lasting results. There is only one thing they can do: concentrate all the love they have in themselves and rise higher and higher. Then, all the luminous beings of the invisible world will step aside as they pass, saying, 'Let these beings through. They carry an irresistible love in their hearts, and we are going to help them express it.'

Notes

1. See *The Powers of Thought,* Izvor Coll. n° 224, chap. 12: 'Creative prayer' and chap. 13: 'Reaching for the unattainable'.
2. See *Education Begins Before Birth,* Izvor Coll. n° 203, chap. 5: 'A new understanding of a mother's love' and chap. 6: 'The magic word'.

Chapter Twelve

PATIENCE:
ITS UNEXPECTED TREASURES

You are impatient to see all your wishes become reality, and there are so many things you wish for! This is natural. And yet, rather than waiting for the day when your wishes are finally realized, you should carefully examine the nature of your requests. Because what you wish for will eventually come true, and if you lack discernment with regard to what you should ask for, how many disappointments and regrets you will have! Before wanting your prayers and wishes to be granted at all cost, ask yourself this question: 'Will what I wish for bring something truly good for me and for others?' Otherwise, *'there will be weeping and gnashing of teeth',* as Jesus says in the Gospels.

Before asking for anything, you must be certain that what you wish for is in accordance with divine law. If you are really sure of this, continue to wish for it, with the conviction that it will become reality. For earth is the field of all realizations. From one point of view this is very encouraging, but it is also very dangerous, for just as good is realized, so is evil.

There are regions in the universe where evil cannot take hold, but you must know that on earth everything is entitled to become reality. This is also why, faced with all the crimes that are committed and all the misfortunes that befall humanity, it is useless to ask the question: 'Why does God allow such things?' It isn't a question of permission; it is the nature of things. It is this way because we are on earth, a place where everything has the right to be realized, good as well as evil.

We must therefore develop patience where both good and evil are concerned: patience to endure the machinations of evil that cause us to suffer and patience to wait for the good things we wish for. But patience is a quality that is difficult to acquire and even more difficult to understand. We can explain it by going back to its etymology, the Latin verb patior, which means 'to withstand, endure, suffer'. So does being patient mean you endure everything passively, without reacting? No, this isn't patience. I will try to shed some light on this question.

Patience is the greatest manifestation of love. In Bulgaria, the word for patience is tarpénié, and the word delgotarpénié refers to the patience of God. God is called delgotarpelniv, which translates as 'long-suffering' (deleg means 'long') or 'forbearance'. 'Forbearance' is not a word we hear often, but it is the best word to express God's infinite patience. Let us turn our attention for a few minutes to this wonderful patience.

For millions and millions of years, God has been waiting for stones to become human beings, and nothing can disturb his peace. He puts up with everything; he doesn't stir even when he sees so many ill-intentioned creatures committing crimes and devastating the world he has created. There is nothing more disconcerting, more incomprehensible than this patience. There is only one way to understand it: you must do everything possible to come close to it, for no definition, however erudite, can lead us to an understanding of God's mysterious forbearance, which is the expression of his love.

God loves all his creatures, and the symbol of this love is the sun, whose blessings of life, warmth and light are received day and night by everyone without exception. But a wolf uses the sun's blessings in order to attack the sheep, while the sheep prepares nutritious milk. Similarly, while a criminal looks for ways to harm others, a saint thinks only of helping them. Like the light, warmth and life of the sun, God's love doesn't produce identical results in all his creatures. If a criminal plots his or her crimes, does that mean that God, the divine sun, inspires criminal acts? No, it means the criminal is misusing God's love.

Of course it is surprising that the wicked, the violent, the usurpers often continue to live tranquil and even happy lives, or at least appear to. It is at this point that some people begin to say to themselves, 'If God existed, he wouldn't tolerate such injustice and such cruelty.'[1] And those who have kept their faith in spite of everything are constantly questioning and tormenting themselves. Unless you try to understand the boundless patience of God, you risk falling into great errors. And in order to understand it, you must never lose sight of the law that is one of the foundations of creation: the law of cause and effect.

There is no such thing as a phenomenon without consequences, and every phenomenon, every event, is the consequence of a cause. Causes and consequences are inextricably linked. But the span of an earthly life is too limited for us to observe this vast game of cause and effect. If we lived a lot longer, we would witness the consequences of certain causes, and we would then observe that the guilty are ultimately and inevitably punished and the good justly rewarded, if not immediately then later on.

We will no longer be here to see the consequences that some of the causes will bring about; similarly, we observe facts today that are consequences of causes going way back before our present lifetime. This means that during the course of a single earthly life we are faced with situations that are in some cases causes and in others consequences, and we don't know how to untangle them. That is why so many events appear completely disjointed and devoid of meaning.

You note an event that happened yesterday or today, but you don't know what may have given rise to it, and often you won't find the cause where you are looking for it, since so many facts remain unknown or misunderstood! Also, the work of historians is often limited to making observations, and even if they try to study how certain events are connected, who can claim to know what really took place in the hearts and minds of the people who initiated these events? So many decisions have been made and executed in secret! So many lies have been told by those with an interest in concealing these schemes! And so many others have had an interest in peddling these lies! From time to time, documents surface and astounding discoveries are made, requiring certain judgements to be revised. But for human beings, their own history will always remain in part an enigma.

You will be astonished if I tell you that a true understanding of human history is reserved for those who are infinitely patient, for beings who never die. And yes, they exist! There are immortal spirits charged with the task of recording all the events that take place in the universe and, therefore, on earth. Although this seems impossible to believe, it is true, but it concerns realities of another dimension.

It is the brevity of their existence, then, that prevents human beings from having a correct perspective and understanding of events: the causes and consequences escape them, and this is why they are impatient. Patience is a virtue acquired as a result of an awareness of the long term. Until you have acquired this awareness, you will be impatient and defiant. You will draw premature conclusions and see only aberrations and injustice everywhere: the wicked unpunished, the good unrewarded, misfortunes that rain down on the innocent and happiness on those who have done nothing to deserve it. Those who are patient and understand the workings of the law of cause and effect see the opposite: that everything is just and everything has meaning.

You will say, 'Yes, of course, we can see that, we can understand, but where and how can we find the strength to bear it?' Through love. Patience brings justice and love together; it reconciles them and harmonizes their opposing tendencies. Justice is implacable, whereas love is forgiving and merciful. Patience allows you to understand the workings of justice: how it punishes criminals and brings victims comfort far beyond anything they have temporarily suffered.

But knowing that the wicked will one day be punished for their faults should not prevent you from loving them.[2] Yes, you must love them as creatures of God, who are advancing with difficulty along the path of evolution. This idea will help you tolerate them. Observe yourself: when people you love make mistakes, you know how to be patient and indulgent, whereas when it concerns people you don't like, even their good actions exasperate and irritate you, to the point where you attribute suspect motives to their behaviour. Only love can give you patience and open your eyes to the intentions of others.

Patience is also a manifestation of strength. Those who are strong don't allow themselves to be undermined by the behaviour of people around them, whereas those who are weak cannot tolerate anything; the slightest annoyance and they are beside themselves. You see people flying into unbelievable rages over the tiniest details! And these are often the very people who remain almost indifferent to the monstrous injustices others have to endure. What people can or cannot tolerate – for me this is a criterion; I see where they are on the path of evolution.

You will say, 'But shouldn't there be limits to our patience? Do we have to put up with everything?' One day I asked Master Peter Deunov this question, and this is what he replied: 'If someone climbs on your back, you must be patient; if they throw swarms of flies and mosquitoes over you, you must be patient. But if they threaten your eyes, if they put their hands over your eyes when you are setting out, this you must not accept.'

What does this mean? It means that in everyday life we must try to carry the burdens others put on our backs, and we must also be patient if they complicate our life and are unfair to us. The only thing we must not accept is their efforts to prevent us from seeing the right path and following it. We must not be patient with those who attempt, through their words or behaviour, to destroy the temple of God within us, to extinguish our light, to cut our links with the Creator. In this case, we must fight back with all our might.[3]

You will benefit a great deal if you really try to understand this virtue of patience and put it into practice. When your personal interests are threatened, by which I mean your comfort, your well-being, your reputation, you must be patient, and not only must you be patient, you must thank heaven for the opportunity to show you are intelligent. You must even laugh at the naivety of those who believe they are able to harm or dominate you, when in fact they are enabling you to have a better understanding of things and forcing you to focus on what is essential. How many times have I laughed inwardly to see people busy creating problems for me and, what is more, imagining I don't notice! I let them do what they want, and I merely try to go within myself, to a place where they cannot gain access.

If, out of a need to increase their territory or influence, people try to interfere in your affairs or oust you, know that you always have the option of projecting yourself into the heights or the depths of your being. And once you are there, never let them in; defend yourself, for your inner space is that of the Divinity. You need not defend your personal, selfish interests, but you must defend the divine right in you. In other words, you must never agree to break the rules of love, wisdom and truth by participating in anything that could compromise your efforts to perfect yourself or the efforts of others.

'If someone threatens your eyes, if they put their hands over your eyes when you set out on the path, you must not accept it.' Our eyes are the symbol of a sacred and divine place that must be respected and protected, because it is through them that we receive the light. Don't we refer to a beloved person or a precious object in our care as 'the apple of our eye'? You have every right to show your impatience when your eyes, your inner life, your divine life, are threatened. So, while reflecting on the experiences you have had, on the people you have met and your current situations, try to understand when you should show patience and when you should refuse what others are attempting to impose on you.

Everywhere we see people looking on silently as the forces of evil accomplish their work of destruction on others, and yet as soon as their own interests are in danger they mobilize an entire army. One day they will be judged very severely for this. Divine justice will reproach them: 'You protested against the slightest injustice done to you, and at the same time you remained impassive before all the dreadful things others were suffering. In some way you have added to their suffering.' And it will be useless for them to try to justify themselves by saying, 'I didn't know'. They should have known.

People try to arrange things for themselves by claiming they have a right to them. But they must put all that to one side. Those who always want to assert their rights make a great deal of noise and often prove to be as unjust as those they complain about, and sometimes even more so. You are following a spiritual teaching in order to learn the best way to deal with your issues, for you can be sure that in the future the present codes of justice will no longer be valid. The courts will no longer give much consideration to the complaints filed by those claiming there has been damage to their personal interests. On the other hand, they will respond right away to the requests of those defending the common interest, the divine right. You must be patient while you are waiting for this to come about, and remember that even if divine justice takes a long time to assert itself, it does exist and will manifest sooner or later.

However, it is important not to confuse patience with the absence of an external reaction. There are certain actions, certain words that exasperate you, and you don't respond, you keep silent, but inwardly you are boiling over with anger or indignation. This is often the case when you have to submit to the authority of a superior: even if he or she is abusive, you endure it without saying anything, knowing that if you react you will only aggravate the situation. But it gnaws away at you. Well, this isn't patience. True patience is accompanied by a sense of strength and peace.

Patience has never been a widely practised virtue and is even less so in our times. The way people understand life today and this need for everything to go faster and faster mean that patience is thought of as a hindrance, and patient people are considered stupid, spineless and sluggish. What do those immersed in business affairs or other activities say about patient people? They treat them quite simply as ruminants. Competent people must always look as if they are in a hurry: in a hurry to get something done, in a hurry to succeed. They must outstrip their rivals, they must be first to gain a position, no matter what damage they may do to those around them… But they also do damage to themselves. This tension, this haste can only have terrible consequences: agitation, irritability and so on. A Bulgarian proverb says: 'Only those who know how to wait until the end are saved!'

So make the effort to wait until the end. How? By sincerely wishing to acquire this quality of patience. Observe yourself; even though at times you say, 'Oh! I should have been more patient… I should be better at putting up with this or that', in actual fact, when you lose your patience you always find an excuse. So begin by never justifying your lack of patience, and then concentrate on this virtue. Think of the creatures that represent patience in different traditions, such as the cow, the ant, the fish, the tortoise and the elephant.

You will say, 'But these are animals!' Yes, it's true, they are animals, but these creatures of God can also teach us something. It isn't for nothing that certain religions have raised animals to the level of deities. These animals represent particular qualities, certain character traits that awaken an echo in human beings. And Jesus, who said, *'Be perfect as your heavenly Father is perfect,'* also said, *'Be as wise as serpents and as simple as doves.'*

Think, too, of a rock that is exposed to bad weather or of a tree growing slowly as it sinks its roots deep into the earth. A fruit tree allows its branches to be pruned every year without complaining, which is why it produces succulent fruit.

And even if they are rare, there are people who are patient. Follow their example; study everything they have had to endure and how they have reacted. Patience is one of the positive qualities of Saturn, symbolized by the old man who has experienced a great deal, meditated a great deal and understood a great deal. Obviously, we cannot expect much patience from children; it is a quality that comes with age, and even great age. Old people who are impatient show they have not learned much from life.

Patience possesses wonderful powers. Be patient and you will live for a long time. You will say, 'But that isn't possible; you have to expend so much energy putting up with difficult people and situations!' No, on the contrary, it is when you are impatient that you waste the most energy.[4] Serenity and patience enhance vitality and prolong life. People who explode and then exclaim, 'Ah! I feel better!' don't realize that this 'better' is in fact a great loss. They should analyse themselves to discover what it is in them that feels better: their higher nature or their lower nature. And a moment later, thinking back on their outburst, are they really pleased with themselves? Don't they feel it would have been better to control themselves?

Try to experience for yourself how effective the virtue of patience is. Rather than resorting to all sorts of syrups, potions, elixirs and other concoctions, drink patience! It will revive your life forces, forces you never imagined… Patience works over time, and in time everything you have lived can become a source of enrichment and joy, for nothing happens without a reason; everything has meaning, but it is up to you to discover it. And the moment you experience suffering of any kind, don't allow your thoughts to stay there, bound to it; project them into the future, telling yourself you will soon forget whatever it was that was so hurtful to you today. And if you simply cannot forget it, you will at least see it in a new light.

I can give you still other exercises, such as washing your hands and then touching your ears, slowly pulling downwards on the lobes. Or you can massage your solar plexus in a clockwise direction.[5]

But don't wait until you have to pass through difficult conditions or suffer great losses and misfortunes before practising patience. You lack patience in everyday life, and this works against the manifestation of all your good qualities. Every day you must work to gain a little more ability to endure things. In other words, instead of immediately reacting to someone's words or to events, become quiet inside, breathe deeply and call upon all the forces of peace, light and harmony: they will help you find the best attitude.[6]

It is so important to work with the breath! This is also why, when you do the breathing exercises in the morning, it is useful to repeat inwardly the word 'patience', immersing yourself in its meanings, its vibrations, its aura. And while saying this word, add an image that will increase its power, so that this virtue will eventually permeate your entire consciousness.

Notes

1. See *Love Greater Than Faith,* Izvor Coll. n° 239, chap. 7: 'Never abandon your faith in good'.
2. See *Vie et Travail à l'École Divine,* Part II, Complete Works, vol. 31, chap. 8: 'Comment dépasser la notion de justice'.
3. See *Youth: Creators of the Future,* Izvor Coll. n° 233, chap. 2: 'The foundation stone of life: faith in a Creator', chap. 3: 'A sense of the sacred', chap. 9: 'Recognize the aspirations of soul and spirit' and chap. 10: 'The divine world, our own inner world'.
4. See *Cosmic Balance,* Izvor Coll. n° 237, chap. 11-III: 'The straight line and the curved line'.
5. See *Man's Subtle Bodies and Centres,* Izvor Coll. n° 219, chap. 3: 'The Solar Plexus'.
6. See *Respiration,* Brochure 303.

Chapter Thirteen

AND ALL BEINGS WILL FOLLOW YOU ON THIS PATH OF JOY

Most people maintain that nothing is more precious to them than having family and friends, than living in harmony with those around them. And yet families are fraught with so much conflict, and so many friendships, unions and associations eventually break down. Why? Because people tend to impose their own tastes and opinions, but their tastes and opinions rarely coincide, even within a family. You will say we don't choose our family, whereas in the case of our husband, wife or friends we choose people for whom we feel an affinity. Well, why are there so many ruptures here as well, leaving both sides bruised and broken?

We are all spontaneously attracted to certain people, because we find them congenial, pleasant, amusing, original or seductive, or sometimes we don't even know why, and this attraction has nothing to do with their moral worth. This is natural. But it must not prevent us from trying to become better acquainted with the people we want to associate with, because friendship and love are based on trust, and if you don't know what you can depend on in others, you cannot count on a lasting friendship or love.

Before you establish a relationship with someone, ask yourself what is solid and stable in this person.[1] People possess different qualities and virtues, which they manifest more or less according to circumstances. But each person will manifest certain qualities no matter what happens. Try to discover what these are so you know what you can count on. As for peoples' faults, they needn't prevent you from having affection for them, but you must be aware of them as well if you are to avoid exposing yourself to disappointment and misunderstanding.

So don't engage in a relationship based merely on a feeling of attraction, or if you do, know what to expect. It will be useless to complain to everyone afterwards that such and such a person disappointed you. Do you want to love and be loved? This is absolutely normal! But if you want love to be a constant cause for joy, both for you and for those who love you, at least learn how to choose your relationships and, above all, how to preserve them. And to preserve them, you must be particularly careful about the words you use. Sometimes a few negative words are enough to destroy years of good relations. It demands an effort, of course, but try to keep a scrupulous watch over your every word, as each and every word leaves traces.

People say, 'I'm honest, I say what I think, especially to my friends.' They demolish everything in their path and then are astonished when they lose their friends! Honesty is certainly a quality, but there is nothing to be proud of in this kind of honesty. Do these people ever stop to ask themselves whether they are right in their opinions? No. And besides, why should they? Isn't freedom of thought one of humanity's great, hard-won prizes? Over the centuries, how many men and women have fought for this freedom to be recognized!

That's fine, freedom of thought is a precious thing, but only if you know what thought really is. So many people consider thought to be any of their mental agitations whatsoever about everything they like or dislike! But they are mistaken! True thought doesn't even begin on the mental plane but on the causal plane, the plane of the great eternal laws. The first idea or impression that occurs to someone is not a thought, and many who claim to say what they think should understand that, if they were truly thinking, they would keep quiet or speak only after asking themselves what their opinion is worth.

Do you want to maintain good relations with your family, friends and others around you? Do you want to be happy with them and them to be happy with you? Then pay attention to what you say. And when you have to deal with someone close to you on a delicate matter, think carefully about it first. Moreover, whatever the subject, in general it is advisable to weigh your words carefully and, above all, not to respond with a quick retort. Because often, when you speak without having taken the time to reflect, you forget almost immediately what you have said. But the people you have addressed don't forget.

Years ago I encountered a strange phenomenon. Nearly every day I heard complaints about a certain sister in our Brotherhood. She was very impulsive and was always making criticisms. One day I decided to intervene. I explained to her that her behaviour was provoking discontent and disharmony. But as it turns out, she didn't understand me: she looked at me with an air of astonishment (I could see from her expression that she was truly surprised) and exclaimed, 'But I don't know why they make such a fuss! Once I've said what I have to say, it's finished, I forget it, I don't think about it any more…' Because she forgot about it, she didn't understand why others remembered, so they were the ones in the wrong! I was astounded by this lack of awareness.[2]

Human relationships, whether between family members, friends, colleagues or even strangers, are very complicated things, in which, more often than not, people suffer and cause others to suffer. If you want to preserve harmony and good relations, it is important to forget yourself a little, to stop endlessly pushing your own point of view and tastes to the fore and instead show understanding, tolerance and patience. This is a sacrifice. But sacrifice is a force; yes, this is the great idea to which you must bow. Of course, there is something in you that will protest, because sacrifice implies constraints, losses. But know that it is only your lower nature that suffers; your higher nature rejoices.[3]

When you stop relating everything to yourself, to your own opinions, feelings and desires, you can begin to nurture a noble and luminous ideal, and this ideal will absorb and devour the thousand and one problems you encounter every day in your relationships with others. Make these efforts, and one day you won't even experience these difficulties, and even if you do, not only will they not affect you but, by overcoming them, you will further enrich your knowledge of human beings, and you will be better able to help them.

One day, I received a visit from a woman who confided in me that she no longer knew what to do with her husband. He was a constant source of irritation, she told me, and not only had she heaped criticism and insults on him, she had actually hit him! I expect you're surprised; it is generally the other way around. So, she criticized and struck her husband, who apparently didn't react much. I never met him, but I came to understand that psychologically he was very fragile.

I began by making this woman see how cruel and ineffective her behaviour was, and she promised to change. But she didn't. She said to me, 'I suspect he has a mistress; what do you think?' How could I have an opinion on such a subject? I don't spend my time looking into crystal balls and reading cards to divine a husband's or wife's infidelities. And in any case, if I had known that her husband was unfaithful to her, I wouldn't have told her. I simply explained that by constantly asking this sort of question, not only was she was harming her husband, she was also destroying something in herself. And I advised her to occupy her mind with other subjects, to read, study music or learn a foreign language. There are so many interesting possibilities in life! But no, it was always her husband and herself… herself and her husband. What can you do with people who make life impossible for others and become their own tormentors?

One's personal life is something so minuscule, so you must stop making it your central concern. What are your little problems in comparison with the immensity and wealth of the life offered by a spiritual teaching? If you stay focused forever on yourself, on your likes or dislikes, on what does or doesn't suit you, you will never really get to work, and you will remain buried under a pile of insignificant things. Stop behaving as though everything revolved around yourself, your partner, your children, your friends and neighbours… Do you think the stars are focused on your family or your social life? It is up to you to turn your attention towards the stars. You will feel better for it, and others will, too.[4]

Once you seriously begin to study a spiritual teaching and to meditate and pray, you will see reality in a different light, for you will have some distance on people and situations. And then, not only will you become less obsessed with the weaknesses and limitations of others, you will also discover in them qualities you had never noticed. Paradise on earth doesn't exist, and wherever you go, even in the best places, you will find imperfect people and reasons to complain. If this is all you choose to see, then of course you will find something to annoy and upset you every day. Yes, but peculiar to human beings is their ability to rise above their conditions. Their inner life is a territory with potential for endless development.

You often hear people say, 'So and so? Oh I've stopped talking to him!' and then they enumerate all their various justifications for no longer even saying hello. And they say this in a very self-satisfied tone, as though their decision was something to be proud of. In this same way, they come into conflict with colleagues, neighbours, friends and even members of their family. No, these rifts are nothing to be proud of. On the contrary, it is by trying to improve our relationships with those around us that we develop the true force on which our own success depends.

There is a criterion that will allow you to see where you are in your inner evolution. This criterion is your capacity to rejoice in everything good that happens to others.

In general it is difficult to delight in the success and happiness of others, especially when they have succeeded where one has failed. On the other hand, people are generous when they see others in adversity. It is then that positive feelings awaken in them: pity, compassion, the need to console them and help them. We even see this in families, where brothers and sisters are jealous of each other and try to outshine each other. But if one of them falls ill, has an accident or is the victim of an injustice, they usually forget their rivalry and gather around to help and support their sibling.

Humans are extraordinary! You would say that, for positive feelings to be awakened in them, they need to see others suffer. You even come across cases where people torment members of their own family or friends, just so they can then console them. They need to see them cry and break down before they feel an impulse of generosity towards them.

I have also seen mothers who couldn't stand seeing their daughter become a pretty adolescent attracting everyone's attention. Some even set about cruelly giving their daughters complexes by constantly telling them they are ugly or awkward. But come their first heartbreak, they take them in their arms, cover them with kisses and promise them Prince Charming!

A woman even confessed to me she was happy to have had only sons, because she couldn't have stood having a young, pretty daughter while she herself was ageing and no longer as attractive. I didn't say anything, but it occurred to me that she was not going to escape suffering, even with her boys. What was she going to do when they brought home pretty girlfriends their own age? Not to mention all the other occasions in life when the beauty, success, competence and talents of others would be sure to offend her.

I know I'm speaking today about something you are all aware of, but have you thought about it sufficiently and decided to keep a watch on your thoughts and feelings? Try hard to analyse what you feel when you hear about happy or unhappy events in other people's lives. Except, of course, in the case of a torturer, a monster, there are very few people who, on hearing about someone's accidental death, would exclaim, 'Great, good riddance, he got what he deserved!' On the contrary, they begin to find all sorts of qualities in those in whom they have previously seen nothing but faults. But it's a bit late; what good does it do them now? But that's how it is; in the face of death, serious illness or serious misfortune, when others can no longer offend them, they become naturally more understanding and tolerant, without even having to make an effort.

So study your own reactions and learn to rejoice in all the good and happy things that happen to others; they will sense it and love you all the more for it. But this will also serve as a criterion for you, and nothing is more important for your own evolution.[5] You will then know you have succeeded in detaching from the astral and mental planes – from your egocentric thoughts and feelings – and in rising to the causal and buddhic planes, where wisdom and love reign, the only qualities capable of bringing you true joy… And one day all beings will follow you on this path of joy.

Notes

1. See *Love Greater Than Faith,* Izvor Coll. n° 239, chap. 10: 'Base your trust on vigilance'.
2. See *'Cherchez le Royaume de Dieu et sa Justice',* part V-2-II: 'Par tes paroles tu seras justifié'.
3. See *Man's Two Natures, Human and Divine,* Izvor Coll. n° 213.
4. See T*he Path of Silence,* Izvor Coll. n° 229, chap. 13: 'The revelations of a starry sky'.
5. See *The Seeds of Happiness,* Izvor Coll. n° 231, chap. 15: 'No happiness for egoists' and chap. 19: 'The garden of souls and spirits'.

Chapter Fourteen

ALWAYS REACH FOR NEW HEIGHTS

Two people meet and greet each other, saying, 'How are you?' 'Fine!' And if they know each other well enough, they give each other a hug, automatically, out of habit. Then, because they are in a hurry, they go their separate ways and a few moments later cannot even remember whether they hugged each other or not. They see nothing abnormal about doing everything in a hurry, unconsciously, even kissing their loved ones, and then they are surprised to find that their relations with others, even those they call friends, are not very rewarding.

When you meet someone, is it really necessary, first of all, to hug them? But whether or not you do so, for at least a few seconds put your mind and soul into this meeting, and a taste of it, a fragrance, will remain with you for a long time afterwards.

Shaking hands, hugging or saying 'my darling' or other words of this kind requires special attention. If it is done automatically, it is pointless, and not only pointless but harmful, as this kind of unconsciousness has a negative affect on the psyche. Expressing outer signs of affection for someone without putting one's mind and soul into it robs something both from the person who gives them and the person who receives them. Of course this 'something' is subtle, intangible, but the elements essential to our joy and fulfilment are always intangible. A look, a moment of silence or a smile in which the soul expresses itself can bring much more than any physical expression such as a handshake, a kiss or even a present.

Real love is a vibration of great subtlety, and in order to emanate this vibration, as well as to receive it, a great deal of attention and vigilance are needed. Nothing is more important than knowing how to give and receive love. Those who have understood this are able to experience such plenitude and joy that everything else pales in comparison. In the vibrant, conscious exchanges they have with others, they discover such richness that the feelings which put them in constant conflict with others, such as envy, jealousy and the need to dominate and achieve social success, loosen their hold. Love is something quite different from the attraction that suddenly propels two people together and then separates them as soon as it ends, enticing them elsewhere.

The day you know what true love is, you will receive from your every encounter the purest, warmest and most luminous elements, elements of immortality, and each one of you will say, 'Thank you, Lord! You have sent me someone who, for me, is like the sun that brings me warmth and light in winter; like a delicious, fragrant fruit that nourishes me; like the water that quenches my thirst, like the fresh air that raises my spirits.'

Listen to people talk (it would be even worse if you could hear them think!): they do nothing but complain about others. They so rarely rejoice and give thanks that these people exist. Humans are imperfect, of course, but beyond all their imperfections there is always something to discover, for within each person there is a divine spark.[1]

You say that what you miss most in your life are friends who understand you, that you cannot find anywhere the understanding you so desperately need. Ask yourself first of all what it is you want others to understand in you. And even if it is your aspirations for the light, for beauty and truth, why do you expect others to penetrate your heart and soul to find out what is going on there? You should be content with the understanding and support of the angels, of the luminous entities that populate space, and of God himself who created you. As for the rest – your sensations, your moods, your likes and dislikes – tell yourself clearly that these are only matters of temperament, that we each have our own, and that it isn't so important for others to take an interest in them and understand them. Besides, are you sure you truly understand yourself? No, and yet you expect others to understand you!

If you complain that people don't understand you, it is a sign you are not yet ready to be understood. Say instead, 'I will try to understand as many people as I can, and I will do everything I can to succeed in this,' and you will soon see the results of this attitude. Others will begin to love you: they will love you because you understand them. And because they love you, they will eventually understand you as well. If you persist in saying people don't understand you, they never will. By this attitude you cast veils over the eyes of others. Stop feeling you are not understood, and these veils will fall away.[2]

It is pointless to demand understanding, love and friendship if you don't first learn where and how to look for them. Are you waiting for them to come to you by way of men and women who will bring you exactly what you wish for? But they are waiting for the same thing! And so, wherever you go you see poor, miserable creatures wandering along life's paths like empty vessels waiting to be filled.

Every being, every object you meet on your path possesses particular virtues. If you learn to recognize them, you can benefit from them. Everything that exists on earth and in heaven can give you something beneficial. You say you receive nothing… But the receiving depends on you: in order to receive, you must be aware and receptive. If you go through life with your eyes and ears closed, with your heart and mind barricaded, you will always feel poor and alone.

In reality, everything can become a source of nourishment for our inner life. Love manifests everywhere in the universe. When you wake up in the morning and open your eyes on the world, don't you sense you are already receiving love? All the life streaming towards you, this is love, a love that flows from the divine Source like a river cascading from a mountain summit. Try to climb to this summit and allow yourself to be filled with this love.[3] When you succeed in doing this, not only will you feel fulfilled but everywhere you go you will spread these overflowing riches around you. And how can those who receive this wealth not love you? They will love you because you ask for nothing; you give. Are you ready to admit that only this way of understanding and living love will bring you love?

Knowing how to love is the greatest art there is. Why? Because love uses scales that are highly sensitive: it places beings and things it wants to evaluate on these scales, and if even a single gram is missing it rejects them, because the moral life requires exactitude. Each of its manifestations must be of the greatest precision.

When you find yourself on love's scales, you can experience this requirement for yourself. If just one gram is missing, you will sense you are still far from love. A gram doesn't seem to be anything much, but in reality it represents an enormous dynamic potential. If you are missing one gram, love will cast you aside, that is certain, for this missing gram puts everything in peril. Listen to violinists tuning their instruments: they must do it with absolute precision, neither higher nor lower than the fundamental tone to which all the other instruments are tuned. If they fail to do this correctly, they will not be accepted in the orchestra.

For each sphere of our life there are also fundamental tones to which we must tune our thoughts, feelings and actions. The tone we must strive for is that of the divine presence within us, which harmonizes all our contradictory tendencies. It is these contradictory tendencies that create so many difficulties both in ourselves and with others.

We could compare a human being to an apartment block of several floors, in which the tenants living side by side are all different from each other and come forward one by one to have their say. Mean and generous, subtle and crude, sincere and dissembling, intelligent and stupid, trusting and suspicious, kind and cruel, optimistic and pessimistic, wise and silly… they all exist in one and the same person. Many people confess they don't understand themselves, let alone others. Just because the human being expresses itself through a single body, people tend to think they are each inhabited by a single entity, and yet everyday life continually proves otherwise.

This mixture of disparate elements that go to make up each human being remains an enigma even for philosophers and psychologists. And yet it is explained quite simply by the fact that, in this life or in previous lives, a human being has attracted different entities. So you shouldn't be surprised to see someone displaying contradictory tendencies. And as regards yourself, you must observe yourself attentively at all times to discern exactly which entity is speaking or acting through you.[4]

Just because you know how to conduct yourself with kindness and wisdom at certain moments, it doesn't mean you are impeccable the rest of the time and that others should always approve of you. Be careful; don't be too sure of yourself! On the other hand, just because you have made some mistakes, it doesn't mean you are incapable of acting correctly. Your first task is to gain a clear view of yourself and then to find the fundamental tone to which you will tune your different tendencies. You will only be able to find this tone by striving to reach the summit.

When you have inwardly breathed the pure air of a summit, if only for a few minutes, you will understand what I am talking about. The word 'summit' symbolizes all that is most elevated in human consciousness. And what represents the summit for one person may not be a summit for another. For some, the summit will be the modest goal of giving up smoking; for others it will be overcoming fear, selfishness, laziness, impatience, greed or anger… This is a daily work. Each of you must give yourself a summit to attain and, once you have attained it, aim for a higher summit. This is how you will find the fundamental tone and enter into harmony with all beings.

In reality, there is summit beyond summit to infinity. Each region has its own summit, which constitutes the region immediately above it on the cabbalistic Tree of Life. *Yesod* is a summit for *Malkuth, Hod* for *Yesod, Netzach* for Hod, and so on, all the way to *Kether* and beyond, for there are also summits beyond *Kether*.[5] *(See p. 110)*

Notes

1. See *Love Greater than Faith,* Izvor Coll. n° 239, chap. 11: ‘As I have loved you’.
2. See *Looking into the Invisible,* Izvor Coll. n° 228, chap. 6: ‘Love and your eyes will be opened’ and *The Seeds of Happiness,* Izvor Coll. n° 231, chap. 16: ‘Give without expecting anything in return’ and chap. 17: ‘Love without asking to be loved in return’.
3. See *Love and Sexuality,* Part 1, Complete Works, vol. 14, chap. 17: ‘Love in the universe’ and Part 2, CW15, chap. 18: ‘Love is everywhere’.
4. See *‘Et il me montra un fleuve d’eau de la vie’,* part VI: ‘Les niveaux de la conscience’.
5. See above, part XI, chap. 1: ‘Malhouth dans l’Arbre de vie: le lien avec le monde divin’.

Chapter Fifteen

SO THAT LOVE WILL NEVER LEAVE US

Most men and women don't know what it is that attracts them to one another. They are aware of an attraction but unaware of what gives rise to it. It isn't people's youth, beauty, wealth or power that inspires love. These assets may motivate some people to spend time with a person, but what they are experiencing isn't real love, for if this person loses one or another of these external advantages, the others will abandon him or her in no time.

What is the origin, then, of this attraction that gives rise to love? Two entities, two energies, encounter each other in space, and imponderable, fluidic exchanges are established magnetically between them. It is this encounter that gives birth to love, with each receiving from the other the elements he or she lacks and has been unable to find elsewhere. We are often astonished by the ties that develop between certain people; on the face of it, nothing should have brought them together. Well, this can be explained by those subtle exchanges that take place between them without their knowledge.

Love is an exchange between two currents of energy, between two opposite but complementary poles. It isn't the physical body that inspires love; this often comes into play only as an outcome, at the end of the process; it merely follows on. Love is inspired by something invisible. People attach far more importance to the body than it really deserves. When the corpses of two people who have loved each other are placed side by side, will they embrace? No, but their souls, which are alive, continue to meet. It is people's inner life that creates attraction or repulsion. Before their bodies are attracted to each other, there are fluidic exchanges that lead them to approach each other. Their bodies simply follow this movement at the end of the process.

Of course, the first thing people notice in others is their outward appearance, their physical aspect, their profession or social position. But these assets don't impress people for long unless they sense that behind these externals there is something subtle and alive that corresponds to what they need in the deepest part of themselves. So if you want to find real love, work on yourself, create something within that is pure, luminous, poetic, musical, and you will attract men and women who are also looking for purity, light, poetry and music. Never forget that it is here, in these subtle vibrations, in these currents of energy, that you will find what is essential.

You meet someone and are immediately attracted to him or her: this person is like a vessel filled with a precious essence that plunges you into a state of wonder, inspires you, expands your horizons and reveals the beauties of heaven and earth to you.

Give thanks, rejoice, and if you want to keep this joy forever try to keep a certain distance at first. Consider your discovery of this being who enlightens, vivifies and strengthens you as a gift from heaven. If you listen to this advice and do your best to apply it, you will never lack such encounters.

Heaven places souls on your path who are capable of giving you joy; you cannot accuse it of leaving you on your own. But what do you make of these people you meet? Do you know how to appreciate and respect them? Do you think of them with a sense of the sacred? No. You try to use them for your own convenience, as though they existed merely to fulfil your needs and satisfy your desires.

Some fruits keep for a long time. As the days pass, their colours become more vibrant, they give off a more subtle fragrance. And although they are appetizing, you don't touch them, preferring instead to nourish yourself with their presence. So when people bring you life, don't throw yourself on them and devour them! Since their emanations are capable of nourishing you, look after them, protect them.[1] This is a new philosophy of life that is worth taking seriously.

When a man and woman think they have discovered things in common, they often decide to live together. And unfortunately this greater closeness can reveal how far apart they actually are, even that they are strangers. Others, on the contrary, feel they are always together, even though they are separated by a great physical distance. So what is more important: to feel the presence of someone who is not physically present, or to have this person near at hand and yet feel such distance between you?

Humans would doubtless be happier if they learned to live more in their inner world. When you truly love someone, he or she is constantly with you, within you, and you live with this person in peace. By insisting on the physical presence of the person you love, you run the risk of constant arguments and misunderstandings. I'm not telling you to stop meeting your loved ones or to abandon all contact on the physical plane but to cultivate more fully the resources of your inner world.

It would be totally unrealistic to advise people who love each other never to meet or live together. But if their union lacks a true inner dimension, the end of their love is predictable. When you feel you are inhabited by the subtle presence of the being you love, you notice that you no longer need this person's physical presence so much. If you feel your beloved's absence too painfully, it is a sign that you have left your inner world, and in that case you should expect to meet with many disappointments. For who knows whether circumstances will deprive you of this person one day? But when you are inhabited by an inner presence, outer circumstances have less power over you. This is the criterion: if you experience as much joy in thinking of your loved one as in seeing him or her, you are free, and your joy will never leave you.[2]

So make sure you are not dependent on the physical presence of those you love: only then will you preserve your joy. You will no longer be subject to circumstances, because you will live in the only world that is truly real, your inner world. As soon as you move out of your inner world, everything becomes problematic, because you become dependent on conditions beyond your control and are at their mercy.

Suppose you are standing beneath the clouds, and you say to them, 'Go away, I need the sun.' Unperturbed, the clouds will continue to darken the sky, and you will remain in the cold and the shadows. When they finally move away, you will feel better, but soon they will return. This is how your life goes: can you predict when the clouds will go and when they will return? No. Do you know how long your loved one will stay with you? You don't know that either. Perhaps one day this person will go away or be taken from you by someone else, and you will find yourself alone, out in the cold.

As long as you remain on the physical, astral and mental planes, you are beneath the clouds, at the mercy of all weathers. So, try to place your consciousness in the highest regions, where circumstances have no power over you. Climb all the way to the causal plane, where the sun of love never sets. Project yourself into the light of this eternal sun. As long as those you love are within you, no force in the world can take them from you. If something takes them away, it is simply because you have positioned yourself too low, beneath the clouds. Climb back up again, and you will find that love has never left you.

The Master Peter Deunov said, 'If you nourish in yourself the idea of love in its most sublime form, you will receive the help of thousands and thousands of loving souls, for love implies the collective work of an entire multitude of souls linked together by this notion of love. Divine love is the greatest force that exists. Never doubt this reality, and the souls that work in its name will always be with you.'

These few lines fill me with wonder: they are pure poetry. We must meditate on them, chew and digest them so that we can give birth to this love within us and vivify it each day. Once we have attained this divine conception of love, we will attract thousands of souls from above, who will come to help and sustain us. Human language is inadequate to express the joy of a soul who has been visited by such love. For such a person to experience plenitude, the mere glimpse of another's face in passing is enough. Never abandon this divine idea of love, remembering that when you love someone it is God who loves him or her through you. So by loving this person you experience the love of God, and this is why the act of loving can fulfil you as much as or even more than being loved.

Undoubtedly you have already experienced this love. It came to visit you, but then it went away. And it will always be like this until it finds in you a permanent dwelling and, above all, the food it needs, because its hunger is great. Yes, it eats a great deal! The next time it comes to visit you, try to reflect on the circumstances of its coming, so that you will be able to call it back again, because, consciously or not, it is you who furnish the conditions it needs. Love comes where there is purity, the purity symbolized by the transparency of a crystal, and it leaves because of impurity.

So you see, this is a very serious question; reflect on it instead of complaining about being alone and abandoned. You cannot lose love when it lives in you. If you feel abandoned, it is because you yourself no longer love.

But we are still only on the threshold of this science: it is with this new understanding of love that true initiation begins. Look for initiation not in books but in the expansion of your own consciousness.[3] If you suffer from a lack of love, it is because you have not yet set out on the path of initiation.

Notes

1. See *The Philosopher's Stone,* Izvor Coll. n° 241, chap. 5: 'Tasting the flavour of the salt: divine love'.
2. See *The Seeds of Happiness,* Izvor Coll. n° 231, chap. 20: 'Fusion on the higher planes'.
3. See *'Et il me montra un fleuve d'eau de la vie',* part VI, chap. 4: 'L'Initiation, un changement d'état de conscience'.

Chapter Sixteen

OPENING THE DOORS TO THE DREAM WORLD

With developments in science and technology, humans continue to increase their power over the physical world. And how can they fail to appreciate all the new opportunities they are given as a result? They are able to travel the planet with increasing speed, to communicate instantly with anyone they wish and to have a house or a car equipped with all the latest conveniences. But all these things that help make life easier can only satisfy a part of their being. If they aren't aware of their deepest needs, there will always be something missing. They will always be waiting for the latest discovery or the latest invention to fill the emptiness they feel inside. And when they have profited from these for a time, once again they will become dissatisfied.

People think they know what they need. Ask them what they wish for, and you will see how they respond: almost all of them mention health, family, a house, a profession, travel and so on. But then why do people who have all these things still feel dissatisfied and unhappy? Because their deepest needs are not those of the physical body, nor even those of the heart or mind, but of the soul and spirit. And these needs can only be fulfilled by the spiritual world. The problem is that people are in the habit of thinking of everything spiritual as unreal, therefore insignificant and even to be avoided.

And yet how many people, if they are honest, have to acknowledge that fairy tales plunge them, if only for a moment, into a kind of enchantment! How do we explain this? Some say it is because it is pleasant to rediscover some of their childhood impressions through these stories. Yes, of course. But the true explanation is that the supernatural is a need of the human soul, and what we call unreal is, in fact, more real than what we are in the habit of calling reality. Everything in these tales – rocks, flowers, trees, animals and so on – is not only alive but animated and endowed with speech, and the forces of nature act with intelligence. And, most importantly, beyond their apparent naivety, these tales describe certain realities of our inner life.

In certain very particular circumstances, when something subtle, unreal and enchanting irrupts into our life, we feel like a tree that, uprooted in the past from its soil and planted somewhere in a hostile environment, now suddenly rediscovers its native forest where it can once again take root and thrive.

This sensation we occasionally experience – that the wondrous, the supernatural, is the true homeland of our soul – is not an illusion: it has its origins in our psychic structure.[1] This is why those who refuse to consider the needs of their soul always experience some sort of dissatisfaction deep within themselves. Even when blessed by fortune, showered with honours, success and glory, they still experience a feeling of emptiness. And it is pointless trying to deny or repress this feeling, for it is there to make us walk the path that will lead us to the light, to the Source.

God can be neither seen, heard, touched, described nor attained. And yet within us there is an irresistible need to go in search of him.[2] It is God himself who gave us this need so that that we would never stop progressing, for it is essential never to stop. You will never succeed in blocking your soul's fervour for long. Even if you manage to shackle it for a moment, it will break its chains and set off again for the heights. And if you don't want to follow it? Then you will experience a malaise, as if you were falling into the abyss. And it is your soul itself that gives rise to this sensation, to prevent you from slipping permanently into a state of spiritual paralysis and death.

So make the effort to follow your soul's momentum by rising with it beyond the limitations of the 'real' world, and you will enter those sublime regions from which all inspiration comes: the inspiration for music, poetry, painting, dance… Some call these regions the dream world… But it matters little what we call it, as long as those who dream are inspired and drink from the divine waters.

We should take the mythologies of the world more seriously, especially certain tales from Greek mythology, for example. One of these stories tells of the adventures of Pegasus, a winged horse that made the Hippocrene spring on Mount Helicon burst forth with a stroke of its hoof. The nine Muses meet around this fountain, and poets who come to drink from its waters receive inspiration.

Let us interpret this myth in the light of the science of symbols. First, there is a winged horse. The horse is one of the symbols of the subterranean world, thus of the lower nature. If it has wings, it means the lower nature has been tamed by the higher nature, and this idea is emphasized by the fact that the place where the horse makes a spring flow is on a mountain, on a summit. The Muses assemble around this spring, and poets come to drink its water in order to find inspiration… This myth is full of wisdom; it speaks of the needs of the soul and spirit, as I have just explained to you.

In the works of mystics such as Ruysbroek or poets such as Novalis or Gerard de Nerval, some people see nothing but phantasmagoria. No, these mystics and poets have simply entered into a different dimension of reality. We can call this other dimension the dream world, as long as we don't confuse it with mere wanderings of the imagination. Dreams, in the sense Initiatic Science understands them, are the seeds of all reality. The physical, material world is only the crystallization of a dream, and if this material world were to disappear the dream would still remain, because it alone is real and engenders all perceptible forms.

Try consciously every day to open the doors to the dream world. It is in the dream world that you will find the elements indispensable for rebuilding your life and giving it meaning. Yes, you can only reconstruct the perishable real by introducing into it elements of the imperishable real. And then, even your face will reflect something of this world of everlasting light, beauty and joy. This is the true life.

The more success humans achieve with matter, the more vigilant they must be in order to avoid becoming mesmerized and engulfed by it. But they still haven't understood this: they imagine they have succeeded in mastering their material world, but in fact it has paralysed them and swallowed them up. This is also the reason they allow their bad instincts to develop – their greed, hardheartedness and aggression.

As I have told you, human beings are the subject of great curiosity for the inhabitants of other worlds, and occasionally angels, also intrigued by these bizarre creatures with their claws and their teeth, come down to make a tour of the earth. Incredulous, they touch them a little and exclaim, 'How hard they are! They feel nothing, they understand nothing, and yet they believe they are masters of the world!' Next they weigh them and take some measurements, so they can decide what zoo they should be confined in. For these creatures will have to be locked up, since they are overrunning the planet, creating catastrophic situations wherever they go.

I haven't attended these angels' meetings, but I am guessing that they will treat humans the way humans treat wild animals. They will put these dangerous animals in zoos, so that future generations of humanity's children can see them. There will be signs on the cages describing their life and past behaviour, and parents will explain all this to their children. Don't laugh: it may also be that one day there will be no trace of human beings on earth, that they will end up disappearing like the dinosaurs, because they behave like dinosaurs.

Of course it is impossible to predict the future of humanity on earth; this depends on them. They have been sent into this world as if into an immense garden, which, instead of plundering and destroying as they are doing at present, they must cultivate and make beautiful. And they will only learn to cultivate this garden and make it beautiful if they maintain a link with heaven, which will inspire them and show them how to conduct themselves and how to work. When I tell you we must open the doors to the dream world, I don't mean we are to take refuge there and abandon the reality of the physical world, but rather we are to learn to work better and become true creators.

Cosmic Intelligence didn't send us to earth with the idea that, once here, we should constantly seek to abandon this world, if only in thought. It designed us to live here in matter, and it gave us the instruments, that is to say the spiritual faculties, necessary to benefit wisely and harmoniously from all its riches. So there is always a balance to be found between the material and the spiritual; you must never forget this. For our physical and psychological health, it is as harmful to try to abandon earth for heaven as it is to abandon heaven for earth.[3]

Under the pretext of praying or meditating, some people run the risk of succumbing to laziness or even mental confusion, for they are no longer able to distinguish the real from the imaginary. You must avoid this at all costs. Even ecstasies, which are the most desirable states for a mystic, will ruin one's health if they aren't experienced with moderation, prudence and wisdom. It is said that God is a devouring fire, and the physical body isn't built to endure this fire for long.

Surprised and even worried by the thoughts and stories their children tell them, some parents ask me to meet with their children and question them. Most of the time I have been able to reassure these parents, explaining that very young children possess a form of clairvoyance, and that when they look at stones, trees, flowers, animals and people, they can see the entities that come and go among them and in them. They even sense that these entities come to meet with them and speak to them; they are like friends paying them a visit. But very soon, the adults around them and their materialistic environment cause the link between the child and the invisible world to be broken. This is also caused by other psychic factors that come into play.

I have also said to these parents, 'Try to recall whether you yourselves don't have a childhood memory deep down, in which nature appeared to be animated and alive, peopled by familiar spirits.' And in fact, my words seemed to awaken some distant memories in them.

For some people nature is open, but for most it remains closed. Or, to be more precise, humans either know or don't know how to open themselves to it. And if they don't know, they perceive creation as a collection of mechanisms, as a juxtaposition of existences with which they have no communication. They don't perceive the subtle vibrations through which all these different life forms communicate with each other. This sensitivity to the subtle, living aspect of nature is what disciples of an initiatic school work to develop.

But there are some very rare beings capable of spontaneously developing this form of sensitivity, the French writer Marcel Proust being a case in point. Because his intuition led him to concentrate on the minute, imperceptible details of concrete reality, and because he knew how to analyse and study his slightest sensations in depth, he sensed and understood the secret language of the mineral, vegetable, animal and human worlds as well as the relationships between them. He experienced their subtle manifestations in an exceptional way. Read his books: his style is extremely ponderous and complex, but he will lead you to a world that is accessible and alive. In penetrating the outer husk of things and beings, something of the soul is revealed, bringing echoes of a world that is far distant and yet so close.

For creation to become eloquent, alive and meaningful, you must learn its language. Your whole life must be oriented towards the goal of entering into communication with an open world and its inhabitants. These inhabitants are everywhere: in the water, the air, the earth, the fire, the mountains, the trees, the sun, the stars… everywhere![4] And they greet us; they gesture to us. But who sees them? And who sees that nature is a luminous substance traversed by rays, the beauty and colours of which no language can describe?[5] If you want these inhabitants to accept you, to help and support you, you must prepare yourself to enter into this immense world with your attention, your understanding and your love. You already live there, you already walk there, but you must open your consciousness to it, lifting the veil that prevents you from seeing it.

If human beings persist in closing their eyes to this subtle world, true poetry, true beauty will abandon the earth. And what will replace them? We will see nothing but hospitals, cemeteries, prisons and an immense zoological park, where animals will be the keepers of other animals. And what animals! The only true art is one that draws its inspiration from on high, in the spiritual world.

Having a high ideal, the highest possible ideal, is the only means of making contact with the kingdom of living nature.[6] This high ideal is necessarily inaccessible, but we need a goal that is situated in the infinite, so that as we follow the paths that take us closer to it, bonds are forged between ourselves and the entire universe. And along these paths to eternity, we will pass through all the stations of abundance, wealth, joy, light and true knowledge.

Notes

1. See *Man's Psychic Life: Elements and Structures,* Izvor Coll. n° 222.
2. See *The Seeds of Happiness,* Izvor Coll. n° 231, chap. 14: 'The quest for happiness is a quest for God'.
3. See *On the Art of Teaching – from the initiatic point of view,* Complete Works, vol. 29, chap. 1: 'On the spiritual work', and *Vie et Travail à l'École Divine,* Complete Works, vol. 31, chap. 2: 'Matérialistes et spiritualistes'.
4. See *The Fruits of the Tree of Life,* Complete Works, vol. 32, chap. 22: 'Nature spirits', and *The Path of Silence,* Izvor Coll. n° 229, chap. 6: 'The inhabitants of silence'.
5. See *Life and Work in an Initiatic School,* Complete Works, vol. 30, chap. 6: 'Matter and light'.
6. See *Le Haut Idéal,* Brochure 307.

Chapter Seventeen

THE LONG ROAD TO JOY

Among all the sufferings you have to endure, many obviously come from outside yourself. But even though you aren't directly responsible for this suffering that is inflicted on you, you have a certain responsibility for it all the same. Why? Because you haven't learned to immunize yourself.

If you are so vulnerable, it is because the negative elements that have been sent to you from the outside world find an echo in you. And due to the impurities and obscure elements you harbour within you, this negativity may even be intensified. If you try to maintain purity and light in yourself, not only will these negative elements be neutralized but the good you receive will be amplified. Yes, if you are not intensely aware of all the good coming to you daily from the visible and invisible worlds, it is because all sorts of opaque matter within you create obstacles to it. So you see, it all depends on you; you can repel negativity, but you can also attract the good and preserve it.

While on earth, you will be continually exposed to attacks by hostile forces. So how can you avoid being destroyed? By seeking asylum in those inner regions where these forces no longer have a hold over you. No worldly situation, position or status can protect you as long as some part of you remains attached too far down in the material realm.

It is true, we live on earth in matter, and this matter is so rich and so diverse that it is natural for us to be attracted and fascinated by it. There are so many things to desire, to possess! And this is where the situation gets complicated. The thought of acquiring this or that object fills you with happiness, but once you have it in your possession you become almost indifferent to it. You almost have to lose it for it to become important to you again.

This is how human beings are: they have wishes and desires, they need to possess, but with each acquisition they lose interest, and their desire turns to another object, and then to still another… This is why those who can afford lots of things should be vigilant, for nothing will ever completely fulfil them, and gradually they will be caught up in a chain of events dangerous for themselves and for others. Matter is an abyss that swallows up those who set out to conquer it without first establishing very solid links with the spiritual world.

Of course, dissatisfaction with what we already have is a great evolutionary factor, since in order to continually acquire new possessions we have to put different faculties to work: curiosity, intelligence, persistence, a liking for work. The advances made by cultures and civilizations are due to these faculties, but we must learn to focus them on acquiring the right things.

One day I met a very rich and influential man who confessed, 'I can have anything I want, but deep down I don't really feel any joy. The only thing that occasionally makes me think I am happy is the sense that others envy my success. If others envy me, it must mean I'm happy.' You see what this happiness comes down to: a sense of inspiring envy in others! And he wasn't even able to take any pleasure in his possessions and power… What poverty! I was obliged to explain to this intelligent man that he should seek joy in the world of the soul and spirit. For contrary to what most human beings do, the more you attain success on the physical plane, the more you must link yourself to the world of the soul and spirit, or at the end of the road you will find only emptiness. In fact, the best thing that can happen to some people is to lose everything they have, so they will have the satisfaction of winning things back one after another.

True joy is not the result of anything visible or tangible. It is joy without a reason, given to us simply by our sense of existing as a soul and spirit. So instead of waiting to possess something or someone in order to feel joy, you must do the opposite: rejoice in the existence of people and things, for the joy you receive from them will give you the sense that they belong to you. Whatever gives you joy belongs to you, while what belongs to you doesn't necessarily give you much joy.

You truly possess everything that gives you joy, and far more so than if you owned it. What joy you can experience before the beauty of nature, a sunrise or a starry sky! And yet these do not physically belong to you. What is most important is this faculty of rejoicing, not the possession. And if you want to taste eternal joy, you must learn to live in your soul and spirit, for they alone have the ability to project you into infinite space and into eternity. Then, even if misfortune strikes you, even if you suffer, you will still feel joy, a different kind of joy.

Suffering and joy… You may say it isn't possible to experience these two contrary states at the same time. Yes, it is possible. Why? Because the human being is composed of two natures: the lower nature, which is acutely aware of the slightest annoyance, the slightest obstacle and loss, and the higher nature, which lives in eternal light and eternal bliss.[1] If you learn to observe everything that happens to you from the perspective of your higher nature, you will discover that your sorrow and discontent can be used as a kind of mud, a fertile silt, which the trees and flowers of your inner garden need for their growth.

Each of us must learn to make this distinction between our two natures. Our suffering affects only one part of us; another part remains inaccessible and free, observing and able to provide relief. It says to us, 'Are you suffering? Well, that is something to be happy about, because if you are intelligent, this suffering will enable you to gain greater lucidity and understanding, and you will grow stronger.'

When people are unhappy, they tend to identify with their unhappiness; they let themselves be invaded by it. This is exactly what you must avoid, by immediately going on the alert and saying to yourself, 'Now there is work to be done. You are suffering, of course, but only a part of you is suffering. Call on the other entity that lives in immensity, in eternity, which is also you. Out of this mud you are wading through, you'll see flowers and trees suddenly appear, laden with succulent fruits.'

It seems impossible to live in a state of constant joy. But in fact it is possible when we understand our structure as human beings, when we know that beyond our physical, astral and mental bodies we possess three higher bodies: the causal, buddhic and atmic bodies, which bring us into contact with the divine world.[2] When we succeed in developing these, even worries and sorrows cannot alter or obscure what we are living in the world of light.

That is why, every day, through our thoughts, feelings and actions, but also through meditation and prayer, we must strive to maintain our link with the divine world and continue to live in our soul and spirit. And our soul and spirit inspire in us a completely different way of seeing and feeling things. When they speak within us, so much pain and suffering is dispelled! It is transformed into peace, wisdom and a better understanding of the meaning of life.

Whatever happens to you that is negative or painful, tell yourself there is something to learn from it. And if someone does you harm, don't try to avenge yourself. Try to find the inner resources that will enable you to neutralize the damage. Believe me, these resources exist. Dig deep, forage inside yourself: not only will you discover unsuspected possibilities but, by your example, you will influence others to make the same discoveries.

Although all human beings are inhabited by a soul and spirit, which aspire to love, light and perfection, very few know how to make contact with them, how to awaken them. But if conditions are right, if they meet someone who can serve as an example and show them the way, they will receive revelations that will gradually show them how to conduct themselves. Which proves that the way in which each of us resolves the problem of evil does not concern ourselves alone; it concerns all others around us as well, whom we influence by our conduct.

Even in the worst conditions, you must never stop working on yourself. And instead of going to settle your scores directly with those who want to do you harm and reproaching them, show them by your attitude that not only have they failed to destroy you but, thanks to them, you are even more alive. This is the best possible form of revenge. So look for joy, this joy of the soul and spirit that inwardly propels you very high, where evil can no longer reach you.[3]

Many activities can be a source of joy to us. But the greatest joy, the greatest fulfilment can only be attained when we merge with God. God has given his creatures infinite possibilities for joy, but he has reserved the greatest happiness for those who endeavour, with their soul and spirit, to become one with him.[4] And for this joy to be perfect, those who have lived these moments of fusion, who have received divine grace, must endeavour to radiate these blessings to those around them, so as to benefit all human beings, to help them, to show them the way, to become a source for them, a sun, a sun that never ceases to give.

Yes, the only true joy is to succeed in uniting with the Eternal and then to have others participate in this joy, to share with them what you have received. Yes, set out every day for this 'foreign land' I have already described to you, this land that is in fact our native country, our heavenly homeland, and then return filled with light and joy. So in reality, our joy takes two forms: rising to the heavenly heights to amass riches[5] and then returning to earth to distribute them.

In the same way that people confuse happiness and pleasure, they also confuse joy and pleasure. What is pleasure? An agreeable sensation. There are activities such as devotion and sacrifice that provide no pleasure but are sources of pure joy. And when you have experienced such joys, whether consciously and voluntarily or not, you will cause others to benefit from them, while your selfish pleasures are of no advantage to others. Believe me, one day you will discover that joy is found precisely where you least imagine it to be, that is to say, in sacrifice, in the renunciation of all kinds of possessions, in limiting what you think of as your freedom.

The greatest joys, spiritual joys, don't really have physical expression, as the highest emotions and sensations are often imperceptible. They are experienced as understanding, as fulfilment, as silence, and they are indestructible. It is these joys that Jesus speaks of when he announces to his disciples, *'I will see you again and your hearts will rejoice, and no one will take your joy from you.'*

'I will see you again…' Jesus was obviously speaking of an inner encounter, a fusion with the divine world. One must study, pray and work for a very long time for this fusion to take place. Why does Jesus project this encounter into the future? Why not right away? Because the road is long; because a lengthy preparation is necessary. But once this preparation is completed, it is permanent, which is why Jesus says, *'…no one will take your joy from you.'* Jesus expresses this idea in another form when he says, *'Those who love me will keep my word, and my Father will love them, and we will come to them and make our home with them.'*

If you don't know how to feed the fire in your soul, it is pointless to call for the divine presence. Even if someone were to give you this presence, you would quickly lose it, for if you don't know how to maintain this inner fire it will die out. Do you want to receive the Divinity in the way that Christians receive the host from their priest? But God is not in the host;

the divine state is something you yourself must produce, earn, win and nourish. What the Church has inculcated in the faithful does not conform to divine law. Why has it appropriated the right to dispense God? It says, 'Open your mouth. By blessing the host, we supply you with the divine.' And in doing so the Church keeps Christians lazy; this is why so many of them remain dependent and weak. No one can ever give you God; it is up to you to find him by striving daily to become conductors of his wisdom and love. And when he enters into you, you will taste eternal life.[6]

You must seek true joy high in the worlds of the soul and spirit, for these worlds are inexhaustible sources. Even if it isn't so easy to attain these higher states of harmony, peace and light, it isn't so difficult either; it is maintaining them that is most difficult. Often, through a lack of attention, through negligence, you allow them to fade, even forgetting you ever experienced them.

You will say you cannot remain motionless for hours with your eyes closed, absorbed in maintaining a divine state. Of course, you have other activities to attend to, which are inevitably more prosaic. But while you are performing these various tasks, you can make sure you don't descend into the lower levels of your consciousness. Keep an eye on this state, as if it were a precious object you were carrying: from time to time you take a look at it to make sure it is still there.

When you go to the bank to withdraw a sum of money, you don't put it in your pocket carelessly with some of the notes sticking out, because you don't want to attract the attention of someone who will be happy to relieve you of them. This vigilance is just as necessary, and even more so, on the astral plane, where there are other thieves who are far more dangerous to you than those on the physical plane, for they never stop trying to deprive you of your heavenly blessings. You become distracted, but they don't; they lie in wait for your slightest inattention so they can rob you of something.[7]

It is easier to obtain something than to keep it; we also observe this in everyday life with regard to any acquisition. So many people who are capable of putting all their intelligence, willpower and patience into achieving success and obtaining what they want then prove to be so negligent and imprudent that they lose everything! Why? If an idea, an inspiration, an enthusiasm arises in you, try to preserve these states, and not only to preserve them but to nourish and enhance them.

Never forget that luminous entities in the invisible world are watching you. They are interested in what you are looking for, what you wish for. If they see that you are focused on what is essential, they will give you a taste of joy that, whatever efforts are necessary to attain it, nothing and no one on earth could ever give you. Guard preciously what you receive from heaven. You don't know how many entities have mobilized to help you receive it. Yes, how can you believe you do everything on your own, without any help?

So from now on, be neither negligent nor ungrateful. Preserve this treasure, keep it safe, allow it to bear fruit, and share it with all the world's creatures.

Notes

1. See *'Et il me montra un fleuve d'eau de la vie'*, part VI, chap. 3: 'Le Moi supérieur. La descente du Saint-Esprit'.
2. See above, part III, chap. 1: 'Le système des six corps'.
3. See *The True Meaning of Christ's Teaching,* Izvor Coll. n° 215, chap. 7: 'Father, forgive them, for they do not know what they are doing' and chap. 8: 'If anyone strikes you on the right cheek…'
4. See *Cosmic Balance,* Izvor Coll. n° 237, chap. 18: 'Union with the universal soul and the Cosmic Spirit'.
5. See *New Light on the Gospels,* Izvor Coll. n° 217, chap. 4: 'Store up for yourselves treasures in heaven'.
6. See *Cherchez le Royaume de Dieu et sa Justice,* part VI, chap. 2-III: 'Celui qui mange ma chair et qui boit mon sang a la vie éternelle'.
7. See *The True Meaning of Christ's Teaching,* Izvor Coll. n° 215, chap. 9: 'Watch and pray'.

Chapter Eighteen

VISITS FROM ANGELIC BEINGS

Benevolent entities from the invisible world travel through space, distributing their light and blessings wherever they go. They may pass by you at any moment, and if you are to receive their gifts and messages you must be attentive.

You have certainly had this experience: you were busy with your everyday tasks, thinking of nothing in particular, and suddenly you felt a current, a presence close to you, something alive that brought you light, peace and joy. And how did you react? At such moments it is important to stop everything you are doing and concentrate on this presence that has come to pay you a visit. These are rare and precious moments, and you must not be negligent and let them slip by.

These heavenly visitors come to teach you, to enrich your life. They are a gift from the divine world, and if you don't stop and seize their quintessence as soon as they appear to you, all is lost. You can search for them and plead with them all you want, but these entities won't come back. Or they will come back, but who knows when… You must hold on to them the moment they appear, for in no time at all you won't have the slightest idea anymore what they have just brought you. It's like when you wake up, unable to recall the slightest image from your dreams; everything is lost. It will be like a dream, none of which you will be able to recall upon awakening; everything will be lost.

I am not saying you have to remain vigilant, motionless and concentrated for several hours. But allow yourself enough time to become conscious of what these heavenly visits represent, so that they leave an indelible mark in you. When the divine world suddenly bursts into your consciousness, there is an unmistakeable sensation, as if something is suddenly opening within you, bringing enlightenment and vaster dimensions to your existence and helping you to continue confidently along the spiritual path you have chosen.

But even if these visits are unexpected, it doesn't mean the angelic beings make themselves available anywhere and to anyone indiscriminately. Even if they are ready to bring help, relief and joy to all human beings, it is easier for them to visit those who prepare favourable conditions for them. What do you do when you want to receive a visit from friends? You invite them for a meal and prepare something delicious. And when you want to attract birds to your window? You put a bowl of seeds on the windowsill. The best way to attract any creature is to offer them suitable nourishment. This is true on the physical plane, and it is also true on the psychic and spiritual planes.[1]

Inwardly, we continually produce fruits that other creatures feed on, both human creatures and creatures from the invisible world. These fruits are our thoughts and feelings. Depending on the fruits we produce, we attract luminous beings or dark beings, for each seeks the food it needs, and what attracts some will generally repel others. So it is up to us to know which entities we want to attract. If we want to receive the support, comfort and light of angelic beings, we must be able to offer them the only food they appreciate: thoughts, feelings and actions inspired by our love for God and our fellow humans, by kindness, generosity and a spirit of sacrifice.[2]

The Master Peter Deunov said, 'Every divine idea you believe in is sustained by luminous spirits of the invisible world. Each spirit brings you its support, each gives you the impetus to make this idea real. However feeble this idea may be in your consciousness, it is inevitably strengthened when these spirits arrive. Yes, for all of space is filled with entities who are attracted by all the noble tendencies of human beings. It is as though we have sent them an SOS and they immediately come to our aid. For them, there is no distance; there are no barriers. They are humankind's invisible helpers.'

We belong to an immense family, scattered not only over the entire face of the earth but over other planets and stars. All the members of this family receive messages every day. But it isn't enough to receive them like the junk mail that comes through your letterbox that you throw away after perusing it absentmindedly. You must study them attentively to find inspiration, nourishment and instruction for the day ahead.

By their very nature, all human beings belong to this universal family, but to truly belong to it they must meet certain requirements. Just as you belong to an earthly family through your father and mother, on the spiritual plane it is the virtues of the spirit, your father, and of the soul, your mother, that have given birth to you and continue to feed and form you.[3]

And just as you have parents, you also have a home, and the home in which you receive celestial gifts cannot be a hovel. I am speaking, of course, of your inner home. It can be a garden, a palace, a temple or a star.[4] It can also be a simple flower, a rose… or a mountain peak. The messengers from above dearly love such places. And obviously, they will also judge you by your activities, whether they are of benefit and use to others.

To explain to you the realities of the spiritual life, about which most people have only very vague notions, I have to use examples from everyday life. If you wake up in the morning feeling out of sorts, and if, in spite of the day's program that awaits you, everything seems confused, it means you haven't received the messages that were intended for you. Why not? Because the evening before you undoubtedly went to some shady places where the heavenly post was unable to reach you.

The celestial postal workers do their job well, but it is only in places that are luminous and pure that they can deliver what they have been charged to bring you. It is up to you to make the effort to elevate yourself to a place where they can present these messages. If, in the meantime, out of laziness and negligence, you have left the luminous regions and descended into lower levels of consciousness where your spiritual organs have grown sluggish, you will of course receive nothing. You must return to this state you have left in order to collect the post that has accumulated during your absence. For it is important to understand that nothing is lost: the gifts and messages you are meant to receive are there waiting for you. It is up to you to go and find them where they were delivered.

We are visited daily by benevolent entities from the invisible world. If we continue to breathe, eat, walk and work, it is because each day they bring us their support. And not only are we helped and supported but we receive elements that enable us to become creators of a new life.

For our part, we too bring help to certain beings, who receive it without knowing where this support comes from. Every living being emits waves, and when we nurture luminous thoughts and warm feelings within us, when we pray and meditate, we send out beneficial emanations, which bring relief to creatures who are suffering. How can the knowledge of such a truth fail to give meaning and joy to our lives? How encouraging to feel we are sustained by thousands of evolved creatures and that we too have the power to sustain others!

Let's say something or someone has done you harm, and you walk through the streets feeling discouraged and devastated. But then you come across someone whose face and expression are so magnificent that you return home feeling relieved and comforted. Heaven has not abandoned you and has sent someone in the crowd to restore your courage. Whenever I encounter such a look, I know it isn't actually the person who has given it to me but an entity who entered this person in order to look at me, and in this look I read so many things! Above all, I read that a world of beauty and light exists where none of the aggravations of earth have right of entry.

Such experiences should make you aware that you are linked at every moment to thousands of benevolent entities. They come to meet you, so why don't you sense their presence? Why do you add to the real suffering you experience by believing that you are alone and deprived of all help? For a moment you felt almost annihilated, and then all of a sudden you regained your strength and courage. So thank all these beings who rushed to your aid. The more conscious and grateful you are, the more you will attract these presences.

It is thanks to the help of these luminous spirits from the invisible world that we find solutions to our problems, the courage to continue to progress and the inspiration to become creators. What we have to live through every day, even what we merely have to witness, is sometimes too painful to bear! If these intelligent and benevolent spirits didn't participate in our lives and help us maintain our equilibrium, where would we be?

I have told you that if we want these creatures to respond to our invitations, we must know what food to offer them. And because angelic creatures appreciate harmony, they are attracted by music and singing. This is a belief dating back to ancient times. However far back into human history we go, music and song have been part of sacred ceremonies. Heavenly entities love music; they are themselves music. That is why so many painters have pictured paradise full of angels singing and playing all kinds of instruments.

Whether instrumental or vocal, sounds have immense power, not only because they can be pleasing to the ears but also because of the power of the vibrations they produce. You are familiar with Beethoven's Emperor Concerto, which has always impressed me with its force and unity. From beginning to end, it is one single movement, carried always in the same direction by one current of energy. Although a variety of motifs is continually introduced, the piece maintains its unity. While in some musical works, the various sections are juxtaposed without any real connection between them, here we feel them flow one from another, like a living, evolving being, confident and resolute, who knows where he or she is going and will not be deflected from this path by anyone. All of Beethoven's genius is here, and when we listen to this concerto we are swept up in an irresistible ardour and strengthened in our convictions.

And the Missa Solemnis… It releases such a force, I sometimes feel my soul is about to be wrenched from my body and pulverized in space. Not only must we become conscious of the powers of music, we must study how to make use of its vibrations, which, when amplified by the feelings of those who play it or listen to it, create an atmosphere conducive to visits from luminous entities.[5]

In an initiatic school, music, especially song, has a great role to play. Since, when we sing, we ourselves are the instrument producing the sounds, singing has the most powerful effects on us, both on our physical body and our subtle bodies. When we sing we emit waves, currents of force, which create forms within us. This is why it is so important that we rediscover the mystical role of singing, focusing all our attention on the melody as well as the words and, above all, learning to choose what to sing.

The spoken word is the creator of worlds,[6] and these worlds are capable of enduring a very long time. We can never tell how long their effects will last. So what are we to think of all this music we are hearing more and more of today, frenzied music, accentuated by violent, destructive words? You must never underestimate the effects of music and, especially, of song.

It is the mystical songs we sing, in full consciousness of their power and with the desire to harmonize ourselves with the cosmic order, that attract the angels. They draw closer and say, 'Here is a place for us'. And they begin to establish themselves in the higher regions of our mind, where they also bring their instruments, their violins and harps… and they join in our singing. When the dark entities still clinging to us sense the presence of these royal visitors, they understand there is no longer any place for them, and they withdraw.

I remember a time when there were still street musicians and singers in many of the towns and villages of Bulgaria. The passers-by would give them a few coins, and sometimes a window would open, revealing the face of a pretty young girl who would smile and toss them some coins. This is a reflection of our relationship with the invisible world. We sing beneath the windows of celestial palaces, and angels toss us coins, which is to say, joy and light.

In the songs of Master Peter Deunov we have such a rich repertoire![7] Learn them and sing them. Sing Blagoslaviaï, douché moïa, Gospoda, 'Bless the Lord, oh my soul', bringing all your consciousness to it, as if you were singing before the Eternal. Pour your entire soul into this song, and the angels will come to collect your prayer and carry it all the way to his throne.

The entities of the invisible world are always ready to bring us light, joy and love. They are gardeners, who come to take care of our inner garden. While awaiting their arrival, we must create a very pure atmosphere around ourselves, in order to attract them but also to keep them with us.

The most favourable time for this work is at sunrise. As the sun gradually climbs towards the horizon, it changes colour. When it appears, it is red, then orange, then yellow, and depending on the quality of the air, it can also take on certain hues of green, blue and violet. And finally it becomes white, incandescent. As it rises in the sky, the sun sings the entire spectrum of colours, each one emitting a sound. And when it culminates in a radiant white, what a symphony!

In this symphony, in this dazzling play of light, our aura is purified, strengthened, and vibrates more intensely. It sends out signals to angelic entities, who sense they are invited to a feast.[8] They rush to take part, and like all guests arriving at a celebration they come bearing gifts.

Notes

1. See *Angels and other Mysteries of the Tree of Life,* Izvor Coll. n° 236, chap. 3-II: 'The angelic hierarchies'.
2. See *Hope for the World: Spiritual Galvanoplasty,* Izvor Coll. n° 214, chap. 11: 'Replenish the earth'.
3. See *Cosmic Balance,* Izvor Coll. n° 237, chap. 4-II: 'Adam and Eve: wisdom and love'.
4. See *Creation: Artistic and Spiritual,* Izvor Coll. n° 223, chap. 12: 'Building the Temple'.
5. See above, chap. 5: 'The human voice', chap. 6: 'Choral singing' and chap. 7: 'How to listen to music'.
6. See *'Cherchez le Royaume de Dieu et sa Justice',* part II, chap. 2: 'Au commencement était le Verbe'.
7. See *Chants de la Fraternité Blanche Universelle*, CD 1510FR.
8. See *Notre peau spirituelle, l'aura,* Brochure 309.

BIBLICAL REFERENCES

Chapter 1

'My Father is still working, and I also am working'
John 5:17, pp. 11-12.

'I am the bread from heaven' – *John 6:42, p. 13.*

'I am the living bread' – *John 6:51, p. 13.*

'Take, eat, this is my body' – *Matthew 26:27, p. 13.*

Chapter 2

'When the unclean spirit has gone out of a person…'
Luke 11:24-26, p. 22.

Chapter 7

Jesus tempted by the devil – *Matthew 4:1-11, pp. 71-72.*

'Be perfect as your heavenly Father is perfect'
Matthew 5:48, p. 79.

Chapter 8

'The fear of the Lord is the beginning of wisdom'
Proverbs 9:10, p. 88.

Chapter 12

'There will be weeping and gnashing of teeth'
Matthew 24:51, p. 124.

'Be perfect as your heavenly Father is perfect'
Matthew 5:48, p. 134

'Be as wise as serpents and as simple as doves'
Matthew 10:16, p. 134.

Chapter 17

'I will see you again and your hearts will rejoice…'
John 16:22, p. 189.

'Those who love me will keep my word…' – *John 14:23, p. 189.*

By the same author

Izvor Collection

TABLE OF CONTENTS

Religion – 6. The Great Universal White Brotherhood – 7. For a Universal Notion of the Family – 8. Brotherhood, a Higher State of Consciousness – 9. The Annual Conventions at the Bonfin – 10. The Universal Dimension of All Our Activities.

207 – WHAT IS A SPIRITUAL MASTER?

1. How to Recognize a True Spiritual Master – 2. The Necessity for a Spiritual Master – 3. The Sorcerer's Apprentice – 4. The Exotic Should not be Confused with Spirituality – 5. Learn How to Balance the Material and Spiritual Worlds – 6. A Master is a Mirror Reflecting the Truth – 7. A Master is There Only to Give Light – 8. The Disciple and His Master – 9. The Universal Dimension of a Master – 10. The Magical Presence of a Master – 11. Identification – 12. 'Except Ye Become as Little Children...'

208 – THE EGREGOR OF THE DOVE OR THE REIGN OF PEACE

1. Towards a Better Understanding of Peace – 2. The Advantages of Unity amongst Nations – 3. Aristocracy and Democracy – 4. About Money – 5. The Distribution of Wealth – 6. Communism and Capitalism – 7. Towards a New Understanding of Economics – 8. What Every Politician Should Know – 9. The Kingdom of God.

209 – CHRISTMAS AND EASTER IN THE INITIATIC TRADITION

1. The Feast of the Nativity – 2. The Second Birth – 3. Birth on the Different Planes of Being – 4. 'Except Ye Die Ye Shall not Live' – 5. The Resurrection and the Last Judgment – 6. The Body of Glory.

210 – THE TREE OF THE KNOWLEDGE OF GOOD AND EVIL

1. The Serpent of Genesis – 2. What Good is Evil? – 3. Beyond Good and Evil – 4. Until the Harvest – 5. The Philosophy of Unity – 6. Into the Wilderness to Be Tempted – 7. The Undesirables –8. Suicide is not the Answer – 9. The Real Weapons – 10. The Science of the Initiates, or the Inner Lamps.

211 – FREEDOM, THE SPIRIT TRIUMPHANT

1. Man's Psychic Structure – 2. Mind over Matter – 3. Fate and Freedom – 4. Freedom through Death – 5. Sharing in the Freedom of God – 6. True Freedom: a Consecration of Self – 7. Freedom through Self-Limitation – 8. Anarchy and Freedom – 9. The Notion of Hierarchy – 10. The Synarchy Within.

212 – LIGHT IS A LIVING SPIRIT

1. Light : Essence of Creation – 2. The Sun's Rays, their Nature and Activity – 3. Gold is Condensed Sunlight – 4. Light Enables us to See and be Seen – 5. Working with Light – 6. The Prism : a Symbol of Man – 7. Purity Clears

the Way for Light – 8. Living with the Intensity of Light – 9. The Spiritual Laser.

213 – MAN'S TWO NATURES, HUMAN AND DIVINE

1. Human Nature or Animal Nature? – 2.The Lower Self is a Reflection – 3. Man's True Identity – 4. Methods of Escape – 5. The Sun Symbolizes the Divine Nature – 6. Put the Personality to Work – 7. Perfection Comes with the Higher Self – 8. The Silent Voice of the Higher Self – 9. Only by Serving the Divine Nature – 10. Address the Higher Self in Others – 11. Man's Return to God, the Victory.

214 – HOPE FOR THE WORLD : SPIRITUAL GALVANOPLASTY

1. What is Spiritual Galvanoplasty? – 2. Reflections of the Two Principles – 3. Marriages Made in Heaven – 4. Love Freely Given – 5 Love on the Lower Plane – 6. Love on the Higher Plane – 7. Love's Goal is Light – 8. The Solar Nature of Sexual Energy – 9. Mankind Transformed – 10. The Original Experiment and the New One – 11. Replenish the Earth! – 12. Woman's place – 13. The Cosmic Child.

215 – THE TRUE MEANING OF CHRIST'S TEACHING

1. 'Our Father Which Art in Heaven' – 2. 'My Father and I Are One' – 3. 'Be Ye Perfect, Even as Your Father Who is in Heaven is Perfect' – 4. 'Seek Ye First the Kingdom of God and His Justice' – 5. 'On Earth as it is in Heaven' – 6. 'He That Eateth My Flesh and Drinketh My Blood Hath Eternal Life' – 7. 'Father, Forgive Them, For They Know Not What They Do' – 8. 'Unto Him that Smiteth Thee on the One Cheek...' – 9. 'Watch and Pray'.

216 – THE LIVING BOOK OF NATURE

1. The Living Book of Nature – 2. Day and Night – 3. Spring Water or Stagnant Water – 4. Marriage, a Universal Symbol – 5. Distilling the Quintessence – 6. The Power of Fire – 7. The Naked Truth –8. Building a House – 9. Red and White – 10. The River of Life – 11. The New Jerusalem – Perfect Man. I – The Gates. II – The Foundations – 12. Learning to Read and Write.

217 – NEW LIGHT ON THE GOSPELS

1. 'Men do not Put New Wine into Old Bottles' – 2. 'Except Ye Become as Little Children' – 3. The Unjust Stewart – 4. 'Lay up for Yourselves Treasures in Heaven' – 5. The Strait Gate – 6. 'Let Him Which is on the Housetop not Come Down...' – 7. The Calming of the Storm – 8. The First Shall Be Last – 9. The Parable of the Five Wise and the Five Foolish Virgins – 10. 'This is Life Eternal, that they Might Know Thee the Only True God'.

218 – THE SYMBOLIC LANGUAGE OF GEOMETRICAL FIGURES

1. Geometrical Symbolism – 2. The Circle – 3. The Triangle – 4. The Pentagram – 5. The Pyramid – 6. The Cross – 7. The Quadrature of the Circle.

219 – MAN'S SUBTLE BODIES AND CENTRES
the Aura, the Solar Plexus, the Chakras...

1. Human Evolution and the Development of the Spiritual Organs – 2. The Aura – 3. The Solar Plexus – 4. The Hara Centre – 5. Kundalini Force – 6. The Chakras: The Chakra System I. – The Chakra System II. Ajna and Sahasrara.

220 – THE ZODIAC, KEY TO MAN AND TO THE UNIVERSE

1. The Enclosure of the Zodiac – 2. The Zodiac and the Forming of Man – 3. The Planetary Cycle of Hours and Days – 4. The Cross of Destiny – 5. The Axes of Aries–Libra and Taurus–Scorpio – 6. The Virgo–Pisces Axis – 7. The Leo–Aquarius Axis – 8. The Fire and Water Triangles – 9. The Philosophers' Stone : the Sun, the Moon and Mercury – 10. The Twelve Tribes of Israel and the Twelve Labours of Hercules in Relation to the Zodiac.

221 – TRUE ALCHEMY OR THE QUEST FOR PERFECTION

1. Spiritual Alchemy – 2. The Human Tree – 3. Character and Temperament – 4. Our Heritage from the Animal Kingdom – 5. Fear – 6. Stereotypes – 7. Grafting – 8. The Use of Energy – 9. Sacrifice, the Transmutation of Matter – 10. Vainglory and Divine Glory –11. Pride and Humility – 12. The Sublimation of Sexual Energy.

222 – MAN'S PSYCHIC LIFE: ELEMENTS AND STRUCTURES

1. Know Thyself – 2. The Synoptic Table – 3. Several Souls and Several Bodies – 4. Heart, Mind, Soul and Spirit – 5. The Apprenticeship of the Will – 6. Body, Soul and Spirit – 7. Outer Knowledge and Inner Knowledge – 8. From Intellect to Intelligence – 9. True Illumination – 10. The Causal Body – 11. Consciousness–12. The Subconscious – 13. The Higher Self.

223 – CREATION: ARTISTIC AND SPIRITUAL

1. Art, Science and Religion – 2. The Divine Sources of Inspiration – 3. The Work of the Imagination – 4. Prose and Poetry – 5. The Human Voice – 6. Choral Singing – 7. How to Listen to Music – 8. The Magic Power of a

Gesture – 9. Beauty – 10. Idealization as a Means of Creation – 11. A Living Masterpiece –12. Building the Temple – Postface.

224 – THE POWERS OF THOUGHT

1. The Reality of Spiritual Work – 2. Thinking the Future – 3. Psychic Pollution – 4. Thoughts are Living Beings – 5. How Thought Produces Material Results – 6. Striking a Balance between Matter and Spirit – 7. The Strength of the Spirit – 8. Rules for Spiritual Work – 9. Thoughts as Weapons – 10. The Power of Concentration – 11. Meditation – 12. Creative Prayer – 13. Reaching for the Unattainable.

225 – HARMONY AND HEALTH

1. Life Comes First – 2. The World of Harmony – 3. Harmony and Health – 4. The Spiritual Foundations of Medicine – 5. Respiration and Nutrition – 6. Respiration: I. The Effects of Respiration on Health – II. How to Melt into the Harmony of the Cosmos – 7. Nutrition on the Different Planes – 8. How to Become Tireless – 9. Cultivate an Attitude of Contentment.

226 – THE BOOK OF DIVINE MAGIC

1. The Danger of the Current Revival of Magic – 2. The Magic Circle of the Aura – 3. The Magic Wand – 4. The Magic Word – 5. Talismans – 6. Is Thirteen an Unlucky Number – 7. The Moon –8. Working with Nature Spirits – 9. Flowers and Perfumes – 10. We All Work Magic – 11. The Three Great Laws of Magic – 12. The Hand – 13. The Power of a Glance – 14. The Magical Power of Trust – 15. Love, the Only True Magic – 16. Never Look for Revenge –17. The Exorcism and Consecration of Objects – 18. Protect Your Dwelling Place.

227 – GOLDEN RULES FOR EVERYDAY LIFE

1. Life: our most precious possession – 2. Let your material life be consistent with your spiritual life – 3. Dedicate your life to a sublime goal – 4. Our daily life: a matter that must be transformed by the spirit – 5. Nutrition as Yoga – 6. Respiration – 7. How to recuperate energy – 8. Love makes us tireless – 9. Technical progress frees man for spiritual work – 10. Furnishing your inner dwelling – 11. The outer world is a reflection of your inner world – 12. Make sure of a good future by the way you live today – 13. Live in the fullness of the present – 14. The importance of beginnings... etc.

228 – LOOKING INTO THE INVISIBLE
Intuition, Clairvoyance, Dreams

1. The Visible and the Invisible – 2. The Limited Vision of the Intellect, The Infinite Vision of Intuition – 3. The Entrance to the Invisible World:

Souls and Spirits – 20. Fusion on the Higher Planes – 21. We are the Artisans of Our Own Future.

232 – THE MYSTERIES OF FIRE AND WATER

1. The Two Principles of Creation, Water and Fire – 2. The Secret of Combustion – 3. Water, the Matrix of Life – 4. Civilization, a Product of Water – 5. The Living Chain of Sun, Earth and Water – 6. A Blacksmith Works with Fire – 7. Water is Born of Mountains – 8. Physical and Spiritual Water – 9. Feeding the Flame – 10. The Essential Role of Fire – 11. The Cycle of Water: Reincarnation –12. The Cycle of Water: Love and Wisdom – 13. A Candle Flame – 14. How to Light and Tend Fire – 15. Water, the Universal Medium – 16. The Magic Mirror – 17. Trees of Light – 18. The Coming of the Holy Spirit – 19. A Treasury of Pictures.

233 – YOUTH: CREATORS OF THE FUTURE

1. Youth, a World in Gestation – 2. The Foundation Stone of Life: Faith in a Creator – 3. A Sense of the Sacred – 4. The Voice of our Higher Nature – 5. Choosing the Right Direction – 6. Knowledge Cannot Give Meaning to Life – 7. Character Counts for More than Knowledge – 8. Learning to Handle Success and Failure – 9. Recognize the Aspirations of Soul and Spirit – 10. The Divine World, Our Own Inner World – 11. Did you Choose Your Own Family? –12. Benefit From the Experience of Older People – 13. Compare Yourself to Those Who Are Greater – 14. The Will Must be Sustained by Love – 15. Never Admit Defeat – 16. Never Give Way to Despair – 17. Artists of the Future – 18. Sexual Freedom – 19. Preserve the Poetry of Your Love – 20. Members of One Universal Family (I) (II).

234 – TRUTH: FRUIT OF WISDOM AND LOVE

1. The Quest for Truth – 2. Truth, the Child of Wisdom and Love – 3. Wisdom and Love; Light and Warmth – 4. The Love of a Disciple; the Wisdom of a Master – 5. Truth, the Kernel of Life –6. 'I am the Way, the Truth and the Life' – 7. The Blue Ray of Truth – 8. Three Levels of Truth – 9. Be Faithful to the Truth – 10. There is no Arguing about Tastes – 11. Reality: Objective and Subjective – 12. The Primacy of Subjective Reality – 13. Scientific Progress v. Moral Progress – 14. Scientific Truth and the Truth of Life – 15. A Fresh View of Reality – 16. Dreams and Reality – 17. Truth Transcends Good and Evil – 18. 'The Truth shall Make you Free'(I) (II).

235 – 'IN SPIRIT AND IN TRUTH'

1. The Framework of the Universe – 2. The Divine Office of Weights and Measures – 3. The Link with the Centre – 4. Reaching for the Top – 5. From Multiplicity to Unity – 6. Building the Edifice – 7. Contemplating the Truth: Isis Unveiled – 8. Garment of Light –

9. The Skin – 10. The Perfume of Eden – 11. 'In Spirit and in Truth' – 12. An Image Can Be a Support for Prayer – 13. The Spirit is not Held Captive in Relics – 14. Speak to the Spirit of Those You Love – 15. The Sun, the Quintessence of Religion – 16. The Truth of the Sun is in Giving – 17. The Kingdom of God is Within.

236 – ANGELS
and other Mysteries of The Tree of Life

1. From Man to God, the Notion of Hierarchy – 2. Introduction to the Sephirotic Tree of Life – 3. The Angelic Hierarchies – 4. The Names of God – 5. The Sephiroth of the Central Pillar – 6. Ain Soph Aur, Unlimited Light – 7. Light, the Substance of the Universe – 8.'When God Drew a Circle on the Face of the Deep' – 9. The Kingdom of God is like a Mustard Seed – 10. The Cosmic Family and the Mystery of the Trinity – 11. The Body of Adam Kadmon – 12. Malkuth, Yesod, Hod, Tiphareth, Archangels and Seasons – 13. The Sephirotic Tree, Symbol of Synarchic Order – 14. Yesod, Foundation of the Spiritual Life – 15. Binah: I The Laws of Destiny - II The Realm of Stability – 16. Chokmah, the Creative Word – 17. Yesod, Tiphareth, Kether, the Sublimation of Sexual Energy – 18. The Prayer of Solomon.

237 – COSMIC BALANCE
The Secret of Polarity

1. Cosmic Balance and the Number Two – 2. Oscillation of the Scales – 3. One and Zero – 4. The Role of The Masculine and The Feminine - Adam and Eve : Spirit and Matter - Adam and Eve : Wisdom and Love - The Mental and Astral Planes - Man and Woman – 5. God Transcends Good and Evil – 6.The White Head and the Black Head – 7. Alternation and Antagonism - The Law of Opposites – 8.'To Work the Miracles of One Thing' - The Figure of Eight and the Cross – 9. The Caduceus of Hermes - The Astral Serpent – 10. *Iona*, Principle of Life - *Horeb*, Principle of Death – 11.The Triad *Kether-Chesed-Geburah* - Sceptre and Orb - Mind and Heart - A Straight Line and a Curved Line – 12. The Law of Exchange – 13. The Key and the Lock – 14.The Work of the Spirit on Matter - The Holy Grail – 15. Union of the Ego with the Physical Body – 16. The Sacrament of the Eucharist – 17.The Androgynes of Myth – 18. Union with the Universal Soul and the Cosmic Spirit.

238 – THE FAITH THAT MOVES MOUNTAINS

1. Faith, Hope and Love – 2. The Mustard Seed – 3. Faith and Belief – 4. Science et Religion – 5. Faith always Precedes Knowledge – 6. Retrieving

Editor-Distributor
World Wide - Editor-Distributor
Editions Prosveta S.A. - Z.A. Le Capitou - B.P. 12
F - 83601 Fréjus CEDEX (France)
Tel. (33) 04 94 19 33 33 – Fax (33) 04 94 19 33 34
Web: www.prosveta.com – e-mail: international@prosveta.com

English distributors

AUSTRALIA
PROSVETA AUSTRALIA
6/A Tyneside Avenue – North Willoughby – Sydney NSW 2068
Tel. (61) (0) 2 8197 1006
e-mail: prosveta.au@bigpond.com

CANADA
PROSVETA Inc. – 3950, Albert Mines – Canton-de-Hatley (Qc), J0B 2C0
Tel. (819) 564-8212 – Fax. (819) 564-1823
in Canada, call toll free: 1-800-854-8212
e-mail: prosveta@prosveta-canada.com – www.prosveta-canada.com

GREAT BRITAIN – IRELAND
PROSVETA
The Doves Nest, Duddleswell Uckfield – East Sussex TN 22 3JJ
Tel. (44) (01825) 712988 – Fax (44) (01825) 713386
e-mail: prosveta@pavilion.co.uk

HOLLAND
STICHTING PROSVETA NEDERLAND
Zeestraat 50 – 2042 LC Zandvoort
Tel. (31) 33 25 345 75 – Fax. (31) 33 25 803 20
e-mail: prosveta@worldonline.nl

ISRAEL
Zohar, P.B. 1046, Netanya 42110 – e-mail: prosveta.il@hotmail.com

NEW ZEALAND
PROSVETA NEW ZEALAND LTD
Unit 2, 212 Riddell Road – Glendowie – Auckland
Tel. (64) 9 889 0805 or (64) 27 356 0107 – e-mail: info@prosveta.co.nz

NORWAY
PROSVETA Norden, Postboks 318, N-1502 Moss
Tel. (47) 69 26 51 40 – Fax (47) 69 26 51 08
e-mail: info@prosveta.no – www.prosveta.com og www.prosveta.no

UNITED STATES
PROSVETA US Dist.
29781 Shenandoah LN – Canyon Country CA 91387
Tel. (661) 252-9090
e-mail: prosveta-usa@earthlink.net. / www.prosveta-usa.com

Updated list 16.02.09. If you cannot wish discover all our distributors, consult the internet site www.prosveta.com

Printed in June 2009
by VASTI-DUMAS Imprimeurs
42004 Saint-Etienne – France

Dépôt légal : juin 2009

N° imprimeur V001751-00 H